Six Simple Rules
for a **Better Life**

⑥ SixSimpleRules
for a Better Life

Practical, achievable ways to be
happier, healthier and more…

David J. Singer

⑥ **SixSimpleRules**Press

Six Simple Rules for a Better Life

© Copyright 2011 David J. Singer/Six Simple Rules Press

Published by Six Simple Rules Press

Design by Sharon Schanzer/Red Letter Day Graphic Design
David J. Singer photo courtesy Myra Sabel

SixSimpleRules.com
Twitter @sixsimplerules

ISBN 978-0615498379

For Marcie, Jeremy, Julie, and Cara

Contents

Introduction

Hello, my name is David, and I'm a learnaholic.

I can't help myself at this point; I can't "quit any time I want."

I learn from books, magazines, newspapers, and electronic media; I learn from seminars and workshops; I learn by making notes and lists; I learn from mentors, family, friends, and even strangers; and I learn plenty by doing — especially when I make mistakes.

Like most people, I strive to make my life better, and this happy addiction to learning provides me with all kinds of great life-improvement ideas — a never-ending supply of New Year's-type resolutions. However, unlike lots of people, I've learned to adopt hundreds of these habits while avoiding the stress, frustration, and guilt that can accompany the early days of January. And we all know that feeling of disappointment: You look in the mirror, take in a deep breath, let out a sigh, and envision a list of abandoned resolutions, hanging there like clothes on the treadmill-turned-clothing-rack in your bedroom.

The fact that so many New Year's resolutions don't last — although they're always being made with the best intentions and with renewed confidence — is evidenced by the perennial appearance of goals like "fitting in fitness," "shedding extra pounds," and "quitting smoking" on these to-do lists (and on so many magazine covers). We've all been there, looking at a largely unchanged list a year later.

That's why I wanted to make sure that this book, *Six Simple Rules for a Better Life*, is not just another self-help manual touting all kinds of grand changes that are meant to impress you — but that instead serve to oppress you, making you feel so guilty that you avert your eyes as you walk past the shelf where it sits next to a bunch of other impulsively bought, unread books, each accusingly calling out to you, *Why aren't you following my instructions?* I wanted to give you a book filled with practical, achievable suggestions for all kinds of ways you can improve your life, along with a game plan for doing so. This way, you'll actually be able to make the changes you want to make. If this book ends up dog-eared and creased, marked up with notes, and recommended to friends, it will have done its job.

✳ Workaholic to Learnaholic

When 1994 began, my wife, Marcie, and I were in a groove. We had just concluded a challenging, but wonderful, two years learning how to be parents and were having a great time with our 2-year-old son, Jeremy. We were also enjoying the house we had moved into in 1993; we were having a great time with each other; and we were enjoying good times with our friends, whom we were seeing again now that we were comfortable enough to hire a babysitter so we could go out on Saturday nights. The only problem was that I was working way too much.

Then, in March of that year, a wonderful, and even more challenging, thing happened: Marcie gave birth to our twin daughters, Julie and Cara.

Instantly, we were back to the days of sleep deprivation (much worse with two crying babies), diaper changes (seemingly incessant with two babies — and yes, I know people have three, four, or more — like eight, for example), and no downtime. Going from one to three kids was a near-knockout punch to our sanity, and I felt that if Julie and Cara had been our first children, we might not have had any more.

Because I was working so much, it was even more stressful. Then, just when I needed it most, a couple of months after the start of that period of madness, I was fortunate to hear a gentleman named Dan Sullivan speak. Dan's company, Strategic Coach®, helps entrepreneurs recognize that time off from work is critically needed for rejuvenation. That sounded great to me — in theory. I had been operating under the belief that working as much as I did was good time management, and I was convinced that working every day was keeping me sane by helping me to stay on top of my workload. Dan's argument was eye-opening and encouraging, and I slowly began to take days off. First, I stopped working on Saturday mornings. I had come to rely on that quiet, interruption-free time at the office as a crutch to help me to catch up on paperwork I would let pile up during the week. It took some effort, but I was able to change my work habits to get the work done during the week. Then, I stopped working at home on Sunday nights, something I had been doing in order to prepare for the week ahead. Instead, I began to block out time for that planning on Monday mornings. In addition, in order to make my days off truly rejuvenating, I stopped reading work-related materials (such as trade journals and business books) and started to read for pleasure.

Before long, I got sucked in and became a voracious pleasure reader. First, I read a lot of popular fiction. (I enjoyed the books, and I also enjoyed, for the first time, knowing what everyone was talking about when those John Grisham and Nelson DeMille books came up in conversation). Later, my interest moved to nonfiction, especially biographies, and along the way I started to read all kinds of personal-development books, feeling myself becoming slowly addicted not only to reading, but to learning.

The transformation was happening: I was no longer a workaholic. I was becoming a learnaholic.

✳ It Takes 21 Days to Form a Habit

While learning is great (and, no surprise, *Be a Lifelong Learner* is one of the *Six Simple Rules*), the big challenge and reward comes from applying that learning to help yourself and others have a better life. If you fail to utilize what you've learned, you'll be like the perpetual student who keeps getting degrees but never goes to work — really smart, but not very useful to yourself or the world at large.

Then again, there's the rub, right? Putting ideas into action is hard for most people. It certainly was for me as well. But then I learned something that first blew me away and then calmed me down, helping me to adopt hundreds of new, positive habits: It takes 21 days to form a habit.

I know that sounds like a statistic that comes out of thin air or from a swami on a mountaintop. But Dr. Maxwell Maltz, author of the self-help classic *Psycho-Cybernetics*, discovered the 21-day phenomenon when, as a cosmetic surgeon, he observed that it took his plastic-surgery patients about 21 days to stop doing a double take when they looked in the mirror at their new selves.

So here's what I did. I *didn't* start every day agonizing over a long list of New Year's resolutions. Those lists are surefire routes to feeling overwhelmed, then discouraged, leading to letdown and resignation, and finally causing you to throw in the towel and give up until next New Year's Day. Instead, I slowed down and focused on one new habit every

21 days. This slow and steady approach is extremely effective and adds up to the positive changes we all want.

Now do the math: If you tackle one habit every 21 days, in three years you'll have formed 52 new habits. Fifty-two! That's a huge number of improvements. The Japanese call the process of constantly making small improvements *kaizen* (ky` zen). And kaizen is one of the reasons they've come to dominate so many industries, such as auto manufacturing and consumer electronics. In fact, in the wake of the massive Toyota recall crisis of 2010, some experts said that the company's woes showed that it had gotten away from the principle of kaizen.

If I were to offer you $1 million in three years, no strings attached, would you be able to quickly imagine all the wonderful ways you could spend that $1 million starting in year four? Sure you would. It's the same thing with improving your life. It's pretty awesome to imagine the great ways your life will be better three years from now after you adopt 52 new changes. Plus, those 52 (or more) new habits will probably add up to about $1 million worth of improvements in your quality of life. True, you can't take that $1 million to the bank, but what you'll get out of those changes will be, as the commercial says, priceless.

✳ Slow Down, Life is Long

Attempts at quick, drastic change are part of the dark side of the "life is short" mentality. Don't get me wrong; I'm a big fan of remembering that "life is short" and that you have to "stop to smell the roses." At the same time, I've also learned that *life is long*, meaning that we have time, and that you don't have to try to make a million changes all at once — which can leave you so overwhelmed that you make none. Instead, if you *slow down to make the changes*, and then *stop to celebrate the progress*, you'll accomplish much more.

Changing your perspective to the longer view will help you immensely. We know from looking back that time speeds by. Yet, rather than taking the slow and steady approach, which will yield fantastic results, we're susceptible to the come-ons of our short-term-focused world: get rich quick; get thin fast; get fit now; quit smoking tomorrow. Almost none of these quick fixes work, and if they do work, they rarely last. Instead, by realizing how much progress we'll make in three years (or even one year, or even 42 days) with a consistent, extended effort, we can let go of that instant-gratification mind-set and experience something extremely satisfying — a freeing sensation that comes with realizing that you don't have to make tons of changes tomorrow.

So instead of being overwhelmed by a long list of ever-shifting resolutions, I began to achieve an incredible number of changes when I slowed down and committed 21 days to each new habit I wanted to adopt. Some examples:

Instead of going on diets that required a total overhaul of how I ate, I made dozens of improvements to my eating habits by making one change at a time. I cut down on red meat in favor of fish and poultry; I substituted whole wheat bread for the white bread I grew up on; I began adding walnuts to my breakfast cereal each morning; and I became a consistent reader of food labels at the supermarket. These changes, small as each one may be, will cumulatively lead to a longer and healthier life. (Much more on this in Chapter 6, Be Healthy.)

After years and years of being told by my dentist and dental hygienist that I should floss, I read about a 2008 study that showed that flossing may help prevent certain cancers and diseases of the heart. That was enough to finally get me to start the flossing habit in earnest. Twenty-one days later, flossing became my newest habit — one which will stay with me for good.

After reading a suggestion by *Don't Sweat the Small Stuff* author Richard Carlson about letting things go (rather than getting angry), I spent 21 days stopping myself from getting upset when other drivers cut me off in traffic. Those incidents used to cause more than a fleeting burst of anger for me; they were always followed by a flurry of livid thoughts as I stewed about the other driver's bad behavior. This habit was not something I could turn off like a light switch. I needed to get used to this new way of reacting, and 21 days gave me the time I needed. Now, when I get cut off, I just let it go — an immeasurably healthier, more reasonable, and less stressful result.

A speech I heard fueled a 21-day focus on cutting down on procrastination — a roadblock to progress for so many of us. I used to routinely put off the more challenging tasks on my to-do list, instead focusing on the easier, quicker ones. Because the "tougher" ones were often the most important, learning how to tackle those first has helped me tremendously in making the progress I want to. (I'll explain more on this in Chapter 4, Be Organized.)

A book I read helped me to stop yelling at my young children and use a more effective and pleasant way of disciplining them.

On and on, I've learned and implemented countless ways to be nicer, happier, healthier, more of a leader, more organized, and more of a life-long learner. Many of these habits, which are now ingrained, began with a focused 21-day effort.

✳ Stop to Celebrate the Progress

The other problem with New Year's lists is the way they can cause us to focus on everything that we *haven't* accomplished. Where's the fun — or even incentive — in that? A list of goals is a *great* thing because goals are the raw material for our progress. But it's important that we don't end up seeing the list of goals as a list of shortcomings, which can be demoralizing.

And toward that end, we also have to make a second list — a list of achievements. Over a three-year period, and for the rest of your life, instead of just looking ahead at the daunting list of goals, it's critical that you *stop to celebrate the progress* every day, looking back at all that you've accomplished. You deserve it.

Stopping to celebrate the progress will help you avoid the perfectionism trap, and put you in a more positive, happier place. Even if you're not someone who would be officially labeled as a perfectionist, you likely suffer to some extent from the perfectionist mentality, frustrated by all that you haven't accomplished — and that's a negative, unhappy place to be.

It's easy for me to embrace the celebration of progress, because I know all too well that I'm not perfect — far from it. I point this out because I used to find myself in awe of the seemingly perfect authors of the many self-improvement/personal-development books I read. Even though I told myself, *He puts his pants on one leg at a time; he makes mistakes just like everyone else; he's not perfect,* I would still catch myself thinking, *How can I ever be as good as he is?* I wanted to like these guys, but I found myself a bit jealous of their impossibly perfect lives.

I'll never forget the moment that helped me get past that problem, as I read the beginning of Stephen Covey's *The 7 Habits of Highly Effective Families.* When I got to a part describing a less-than-perfect interaction Covey had with his wife, I was so happy. *He's not perfect,* I thought, somewhat in disbelief, but mostly with great relief. (Reveling in someone's unhappiness — see, I told you I'm not perfect.) It's not that I really thought that anyone was perfect, but when you read books like Covey's, you can be left with the impression that these writers are superhuman, that they always practice exactly what they preach. I'll tell you right now: I work hard to do everything that I recommend in this book, but I do not succeed all the time — it's just not possible. I *do* continuously make progress though, and that's what it's about — progress, not perfection.

✳ Goal Setting, in Short

People accomplish more when they write down their goals. Not a once-a-year-New-Year's-resolutions list, but a running list of goals — an ongoing list of improvement ideas for you and for the world.

Once you start your list, break the goals down into manageable pieces. For example, "writing a book" is a very big goal. Writing an outline for the book is more manageable, and a good place to start. Writing a chapter for your book is a big goal. Writing a page or two is a more manageable piece.

Just as with a project like writing a book, breaking down self-improvement goals into smaller pieces is just right for 21-day focuses for adopting new habits. For example, completely changing the way you eat is too much for 21 days. More manageable goals like cutting way back on fried foods, cutting way back on soda and other sugary drinks, and remembering to eat enough fruits and vegetables each day are great 21-day goals.

✳ Really Big Goals

In addition to the list that I use for my own 21-day goals, I have a list of bigger goals from which I regularly pull bite-size pieces. These bigger, "lifetime" goals are things that I want to accomplish personally (such as to live a long and healthy life), as well as extremely lofty goals that I want to accomplish to make the world a better place. Among these lifetime goals are the *Six Simple Rules* that you'll be reading about in these pages: Be Happy, Be Nice, Be a Leader, Be Organized, Be a Lifelong Learner, and Be Healthy.

The lofty, "make the world a better place" goals actually have gotten a name. They're known as BHAGs — pronounced BEE-hags, and meaning Big Hairy Audacious Goals, a term coined by James Collins and Jerry Porras, authors of *Built to Last: Successful Habits of Visionary Companies*. Collins and Porras explain that setting BHAGs is one of the key habits of successful companies.

The same applies to successful people. If success for you means being happy, you'll be more successful if you have goals to help you get there; if success for you means being healthy, you'll be more successful if you have goals to help you get there; etc. And the one way to be sure that you *won't* achieve your goals is if you don't have goals in the first place.

My biggest, hairiest, most audacious goal is "world peace." Yes, I know, that's about as big, hairy, and audacious as a goal can be. But what the heck? Why not? BHAGs help me to create smaller goals, including new habits that I can adopt in 21-day periods. While world peace won't take 21 days, when it inspires me to do things like being nicer to everyone I meet, volunteering more in my community, and helping individuals in need, I know that I'm making progress toward that bigger goal.

I'm not a world leader and don't intend to be, so I won't be striving for world peace through diplomacy and politics. I'm going to focus on making an impact in an area where I know how to help — helping everyone in the world to be happy (yes, another huge goal in and of itself). I figure that if everyone in the world is happy, world peace will be an automatic by-product. I admit that's a simplistic way to think, and every time I say that to myself, I hear Elle Woods (as played by Reese Witherspoon in *Legally Blonde)* explaining why her client, exercise queen Brooke Wyndham, couldn't be guilty of murder: "I just don't think that Brooke could've done this. Exercise gives you endorphins. Endorphins make you happy. Happy people just don't shoot their husbands. They just don't." Using similar logic, I say happy people won't be warring people, and thus my plan: World peace will naturally follow worldwide happiness. (You heard it here first! ☺)

So now I have the BHAG of "helping everyone to be happy" to work on, and I'll tell you about my plan for that.

✳ My Goal for This Book

It's very gratifying for me to find that my ideas are helping people, whether it's my wife, my kids, my friends, my co-workers, or people I hardly know. I'm delighted, for example, when weeks, months, or even years after I innocently tell a friend about something that works for me, they proudly report back to me about their success since our conversation — a conversation I might not even recall because it was matter-of-fact at the time, just the passing along of some words of wisdom.

Many people I know have been inspired by me to exercise more. (One couple, for example, reported a few months after vacationing with my wife and me that they were exercising almost every morning.) Friends have told me that I have inspired them to read more. One co-worker told me she had adopted the habit of donating one thing in her house to charity each time she bought something new (an idea I had read elsewhere). Two other co-workers told me they had switched from soda to seltzer with a splash of juice soon after a wellness presentation I gave at our office. And recently, after my friend Larry got a bunch of us together around the holidays, I sent him a note thanking him for doing so, in response to which he wrote, "Thanks to you and Marcie for coming and committing so early. You are a class act. I remember something you told me and I try to follow through as consistently as you — thank people. You told me you always thank the kids' coaches, teachers, or whomever. I try to always thank everyone."

While all of those experiences have been extremely gratifying, I need a wider reach in order to help everyone to be happy — and that's where this book comes in.

✳ Lifelong Learning

In early 2010, I saw Malcolm Gladwell speak. (Gladwell wrote three bestselling books between 2000 and 2008: *The Tipping Point*, *Blink*, and *Outliers*.) If you've read Gladwell's books, you'll probably agree that he's one of the great "thinkers" of our time, and that he sees things differently than most people — and sees things that other people don't see (until he points them out to us). At the end of the program, he took questions from the audience. One person asked, "How can we teach our children to think like you?" I wasn't sure that Gladwell would have a good answer to give; it can be tough for any person to explain how to become someone who thinks like he does. I was eager for the response, however, because *I* was interested in learning to think like Gladwell. He explained that he had a relatively ordinary formal education, including four years of college, and that what he learned as an adult was the key. His conclusion, therefore, wasn't about teaching our children. Instead, his "secret" was to enhance our adult experiences. That hit home with me because it sounded much like what I had gone through. I had a particularly uninspired, "traditional" formal education. Then, as an adult, I became a learnaholic, falling in love with lifelong learning and with improving myself.

This book is a collection of wisdom that I have gleaned from my life as a learnaholic. It's full of ideas you can use — and a game plan for using them. Learning from your experiences is critical. Reading supplements those experiences; it's a shortcut to accumulating wisdom, a way of learning without having to have your own experiences for every single thing. Reading this book will save you a lot of work you would otherwise have to put in searching for the best ideas. You'll read examples from some of the many books that have affected me, so you can decide whether they are books you should explore. If the ones I talk about resonate with you, seek them out. This is not meant to be a summary of the best books, but more of a taste of the best books and ideas — kind of a "self-help's greatest hits" — in the framework of how one regular guy's life and experiences were improved by them.

And so, I propose that you make *Six Simple Rules for a Better Life* a part of your lifelong learning. Adopting even one new habit can make a significant improvement in your life. And you'll get many ideas for new habits from this book.

✳ Please Write in This Book

As you get ideas, write them down. I've given you worksheets at the end of each chapter and I also suggest that you make notes throughout the book (and you e-reader users, add notes and highlights). I write in all my books because it helps me to learn, and I encourage you to do the same. If you want to learn, get out a pen and start underlining things. Start writing in the margins. That's right — you know those areas of white space on the left and right, and at the top and bottom of the page? That's what they're there for. (Of course, if you want to buy a second copy to keep in pristine condition, that's very cool with me too.)

So hurry up and get started — and then *stop to celebrate the progress* of a better life.

Enjoy the book!
David J. Singer
New Jersey, 2011

Chapter 1
Be Happy

"You won't need passports to get into Mexico. But I can't guarantee that you'll be able to get back into the United States when your trip to Mexico is over." That was a scary thought.

On our wedding night in May of 1988, my wife, Marcie, and I stayed at a hotel by New York's LaGuardia airport. The idea was to be able to catch an early flight the next morning for our honeymoon. Also, staying in a hotel on our wedding night, rather than in our apartment, was special.

We got up bright and early in the morning and went to the airport to check in. The woman at the check-in counter asked us for our passports. I had never been to Mexico before, but I had been to Canada a bunch of times without a passport and didn't even consider the idea that we would need passports to go to Mexico. If the subject had crossed my mind, I would have thought, "Mexico is like Canada. You can drive there. You don't need a passport." So, I replied, "We didn't bring them. We don't need passports. We're only going to Mexico."

After she advised us that we could get into Mexico without passports, but that she couldn't guarantee we could get back into the United States, we decided that retrieving our passports would be the wise decision. However, there was no way we would be able to retrieve them in time for our flight. Luckily, we were able to book a flight for later that day. We took a taxi back to our apartment, got our passports, spent a few hours walking around Manhattan, had a nice lunch, and then headed back to the airport for our flight. It was annoying. We were supposed to arrive in Mexico early that day. And this was our honeymoon. Honeymoons are perfect in fairy tales. We weren't happy that our plans had been derailed. But, as Bruce Springsteen sings in "Rosalita": "Someday we'll look back on this and it will all seem funny." Years later, our honeymoon passport "fiasco" *does* seem funny. It wasn't a calamity. It's just a story. One we've told many times, laughing as we tell it.

✳ Everyone Wants to Be Happy

There are numerous books on happiness, with titles such as *7 Steps to Being Happy From the Inside Out*, *The 9 Choices of Extremely Happy People*, *The 9 Habits of Maximum Happiness*, *What Happy People Know*, *100 Simple Secrets of Happy People*, *The Happiness Prescription*, *The Art of Happiness*, *Authentic Happiness*, *The Pursuit of Happiness*, and *Happiness Now!* I've read a few of these, and searching for the names of these books makes me want to read the rest — I'm always looking for more secrets to happiness. And judging by the proliferation of books, Web sites, and blog posts on the subject, I'm not alone.

There are many secrets, methods, and tricks available to help you be happy. The subjects of the chapters of this book, for example — being nice, being a leader, being organized, being a lifelong learner, and being healthy — all contribute to your happiness. And your happiness is definitely something you can choose to impact. This chapter will give you lots of ideas for directly hitting the happiness target.

✳ The Power of Thinking

In 1952, Norman Vincent Peale wrote *The Power of Positive Thinking*. The book's title has a nice ring to it and has become a catchphrase — and it's a great book. But I've learned that both positive *and* negative thinking possess tremendous power — and have a great impact on happiness.

After I read *Don't Sweat the Small Stuff* by Richard Carlson, I read a fantastic book that he co-wrote with Joseph Bailey, *Slowing Down to the Speed of Life*, which taught me the impact that our thoughts, positive or negative, have on how we feel. Carlson and Bailey instruct us to see the link between our thinking and our emotions. You can't feel angry without having angry thoughts, they note, or feel stressed without having stressful thoughts.

Try it. Try being angry right now. How do you do it? By thinking angry thoughts. There's no other way.

✳ Act Before You React

Once we realize the connection between what we think and how we feel, we can do something about it. Because how we feel comes from what we think, and because we can learn to recognize when we're thinking and then take control of our thoughts, we can choose to be happy. How great is that?

As I mentioned in the introduction, this book is filled with ideas for new habits for you to incorporate for a better life. Like the saying, "the first step is admitting you have a problem," the first step to forming a new habit is deciding that you want to change. Once you make that decision, your awareness increases. You start noticing particular behaviors or situations as they arise — like the way you suddenly start to notice a certain kind of car everywhere you look when you are considering buying that kind of car. It's important that you gain this awareness in order to be successful in forming a new habit. That's one of the reasons you should focus on one habit at a time — recognizing that *life is long,* and then *slowing down to make the changes* — because it's hard to create an awareness of too many changes all at the same time. When you focus on one thing, you can slow down your thinking and your actions, allowing you to "act before you react," as my friend Levi once told me — whether that means choosing to be nice, as we'll discuss in Chapter 2, making a healthy choice, as we'll discuss in Chapter 6, or choosing to be happy.

One of the first things I noticed years ago when I started to slow down was that I was sweating a lot of small stuff. For example, my son, Jeremy, had a bad habit of moving too fast and spilling drinks at the kitchen table. I realized that when a friend of his came over and spilled a drink, I would rush to help clean up and would never criticize the friend. Meanwhile, when Jeremy spilled something (for what seemed like the millionth time), my wife and I would get angry with him. How nice it was to learn to slow down before we yelled at our son — stopping to realize that he already felt bad about it and that there really was no reason for us to "cry over spilled milk." This allowed us, instead, to treat him like the person he is to us — the most special person in the world.

These changes take practice, which is why I talk about the 21 days it takes to form a new habit. As the 21 days go by, your awareness will grow. If you slip along the way, or even after, don't beat yourself up. You can't rewind, you can't change the past, but you can, and you will, learn from the experiences, especially because you have that awareness and are open to learning and changing.

In *The Power of Positive Thinking,* Norman Vincent Peale tells the story of a business meeting where tempers were beginning to flare. All of a sudden, one man got up and walked over to a couch to lie down. The others at the meeting were concerned that the man was ill. He explained that he was not, but that lying down was a strategy he had learned to stop himself when he felt himself beginning to get mad — a strategy of acting before he reacted. Lying down would break the tension of the meeting. The same gentleman also learned to control his quick temper by reversing his normal physical reactions — instead of clenching his fist and raising his voice, he deliberately extended his fingers and spoke quietly, because you can't really argue when you are whispering. That's a good habit to adopt.

I've worked very hard to recognize and then control my thoughts. My favorite example relates to driving in the New York area. Before the term *road rage* was coined, I exhibited road rage. Nothing too crazy, but when a car cut me off, I'd give the driver the finger. When I did that, he would almost always give me the finger back. He would drive away and I'd keep thinking about it. I'd keep replaying it in my mind: "What a jerk that guy was. I can't believe he cut me off." When something like that happens now, I just let it roll off me. When someone cuts me off, I shake my head in disbelief and then move on. And the best part is that the incident — and the anger — disappear from my head quickly, rather than lingering with me throughout the remainder of the day. It's liberating to realize that most of our feelings about things we experience come from our thoughts about those experiences. This is illustrated by the following story, versions of which I've read in several places:

Two former prisoners of war get together.

"Have you forgiven our jailers?" one asks the other.

"Yes."

"Well, I haven't. I'm still consumed with hatred for them."

"In that case," his friend says, "they still have you in prison."

My friend Shannon told me, "Always use your superpowers for good." She told me she learned that saying from a dear, departed friend of hers, who had said it often. He meant that we have very powerful minds, and we have to watch what we do with them. We can't let our thoughts run away from us. Day*dreaming* can be okay. Day*maring* (imagining nightmare scenarios) is not good. I remind myself all the time: Always use your superpowers for good. I love that.

I'm no longer a prisoner of my own thoughts when it comes to driving. After a bunch of years of this new behavior, it feels like I rarely get cut off by aggressive drivers. But I know that can't be the case. There are still as many aggressive drivers, maybe even more than ever, it's just that I don't notice them as often. And when I see someone do something particularly stupid on the road, I don't get angry. I laugh at the idiotic behavior. (Occasionally, if a driver does something particularly dangerous, I do get angry, but I get over it fast, and I think how sad it is that that person is endangering himself and others.)

There are plenty of opportunities to laugh about drivers. One of my favorites is when a guy won't let you merge into his lane in a congested traffic situation (we have a lot of that in New York). If he allows you in, all he loses is one car length. How can that hurt him? It's so silly, it's laughable. I regularly see people give the finger to other drivers who squeeze in front of them. And I know that the angry person ruined a part of his own day by being so bothered by the "infraction." (And, these days, you might be putting your life at risk by giving someone the finger. You don't know what kind of crazy reaction you're going to get for doing that.) Another place where people commonly feel rage is airports. Since 9/11, airport rage is rarely tolerated. And there is almost no tolerance at all for rage on a plane.

I recall one time before 9/11 when I was on a plane and a woman properly took the opportunity to board early when the flight attendants called for those traveling with small children. She had four little ones in tow and seated them all together, but not all four seats were assigned to her. She fended off the people assigned to the seats she had taken, including a woman with teens who was upset that she had to move. "It's not my fault that she decided to have four kids," the displaced woman complained. The mother of the four little kids went about things the wrong way, taking seats that were not hers without asking. But the woman with the teens held on to her anger, instead of sitting back and relaxing. She told the story numerous times during the flight — to flight attendants, to fellow passengers on the bathroom line, to anyone who would listen. She let negative thinking ruin her day. (And she probably made people around her tense.)

On the same flight, another woman with two young boys got extremely angry at the flight attendants because she was rebuffed when she tried to bring the boys to the first-class bathroom. She, too, told her story to several flight attendants and numerous passengers instead of just getting over it.

That was just one flight. There are countless similar incidents every day when people ruin their own days by dwelling on the negative. Rhonda Byrne, best-selling author of *The Secret*, says that thinking unpleasant thoughts is like putting bad things into your body. And my friend Sean says, "Bad thoughts are like watching a bad movie over and over. You wouldn't do that. So stop thinking bad thoughts." I'm sure you can see how we can all be happier by thinking more about our thinking.

✳ "You Can't Tell Me How to Feel!"

The power of thinking has also enhanced my ability to help others. In the past, when I didn't agree with how my wife felt about a certain situation, I would say, "You shouldn't feel that way." That sentence is the epitome of my being from Mars, as I learned in John Gray's *Men Are From Mars, Women Are From Venus*. The standard reply from my Venusian wife was, "You can't tell me how to feel!" After many debates on the subject with my wife and others, I finally stopped doing it. But I found it frustrating. I often wanted to tell my wife she was sweating the small stuff, that she would feel better if she stopped doing that. Then I realized that with the way she was thinking, it was logical for her to feel the way she was feeling, and that it made no sense for me to say, "You shouldn't feel that way." What I had to do was help her change her thinking, which would automatically change the way she felt.

Now, my wife and children all understand our common language about our thinking and how it impacts how we feel. When my daughter would say, "Mom got me so angry," I would explain to her that I understood why she felt the way she did, and that while her anger initially came as a result of something her mom did, her continued angry feelings were a result of what she was now thinking. "If you're ready to move on," I told her, "stop having those angry thoughts and you'll feel better." After a bunch of these types of discussions, I noticed that we had become a more peaceful house. In fact, after not too much time, my kids started to help me recognize when *I* needed to mellow out — to not sweat the small stuff.

For example, when Jeremy was a high school junior and I was taking him on college visits, we had a wide range of experiences with the different colleges' admissions departments. Some were organized and buttoned-up. Others were far less so. At one point, I complained about a frustrating experience we had just had. Jeremy said, "What's the big deal? It doesn't matter. You're sweating the small stuff, Dad." He was completely right.

During that same school year, Jeremy and I had an argument late one Saturday night (once he got to high school, almost all our arguments seemed to happen late at night). He said he was going to be home early, and we had a debate about the definition of early. Shortly after we were done arguing, while I was lying in bed still going over the argument, letting my thoughts run away with themselves, Jeremy stuck his head into my room. "Dad, one more thing. Isn't this small stuff? You've always said not to sweat the small stuff. That's why I don't get upset about things. I don't sweat the small stuff." Lying there in the dark, I smiled and said, "You're right. Sorry. I was just annoyed." "Next time," Jeremy replied, "tell yourself not to be annoyed."

That reminds me of another story, which I've read or heard a bunch of times:

A father passing by his son's bedroom was astonished to see that the bed was nicely made and everything was picked up. Then he saw an envelope, prominently propped up on the pillow, that was addressed to "Dad." Fearing the worst, he opened the envelope with trembling hands and read the letter.

> Dear Dad:
>
> It is with great regret and sorrow that I'm writing you. I had to elope with my new girlfriend because I wanted to avoid a scene with Mom and you.
>
> I have been finding real passion with Stacy and she is so nice.
>
> But I knew you would not approve of her because of all her piercings, tattoos, tight motorcycle clothes, and the fact that she is much older than I am. But it's not only the passion…Dad, she's pregnant.
>
> Stacy said that we will be very happy.
>
> She owns a trailer in the woods and has a stack of firewood for the whole winter. We share a dream of having many more children.

Stacy has opened my eyes to the fact that marijuana doesn't really hurt anyone. We'll be growing it for ourselves and trading it with the other people who live nearby for cocaine and ecstasy.

In the meantime, we will pray that science will find a cure for AIDS so Stacy can get better.

Don't worry, Dad. I'm 15 and I know how to take care of myself.

Someday I'm sure that we will be back to visit so that you can get to know your grandchildren.

Love,
Your son John

p.s. Dad, none of the above is true. I'm over at Tommy's house. I just wanted to remind you that there are worse things in life than a bad report card. The report card is in my center desk drawer. I love you. Call me when it's safe to come home.

I chuckle each time I read this story. I love the lesson the 15-year-old gives us when he reminds his dad not to sweat the small stuff (in this case, a poor report card). I don't know whether John was grounded or got some other punishment after dear old Dad got a look at that report card. Either way, I hope Dad saw the wisdom in his son's note. When our teens can remind us how to properly behave, we've taught them well.

✳ You *Can* Choose the Way You Think

In *Learned Optimism*, Martin E.P. Seligman explains that individuals can choose the way they think, which he says is one of the most significant findings in contemporary psychology. Seligman is part of the "positive psychology" movement — in fact, he is often referred to as the father of that movement. His book, as its title implies, is about learning to be optimistic. Seligman explains that people who are pessimistic believe that the causes of unhappy experiences in their lives are permanent, which causes a feeling of helplessness. For example, "I have a terrible life" is a permanent and pessimistic thought, whereas, "I've been having some terrible days recently" is a temporary, optimistic view.

Optimists expect things to work out for the best. That's me. For example, when it was time for me to apply to college, I applied early decision to an Ivy League school. I had no chance of getting in. None. I didn't get in, which worked out for the best. I ended up at a college where I had an incredible experience — I met lifelong friends (including my wife), had a successful academic experience, and was a leader of the school radio station. I've said many times that not getting into that Ivy League school was the best thing that ever happened to me. (I know my kids agree — because I wouldn't have met their mother if I had been accepted. ☺)

Seligman spends a lot of time in his book talking about the influence parents have on their children's optimism (or pessimism). I haven't let my kids be pessimistic. If they are frustrated with their schoolwork, for example, and say, "I'll never understand algebra," I will ask them, "Wasn't there something else in the past that you thought you would never learn?" "Yes," they tend to meekly reply, knowing where I'm going. "What happened with that situation?" I continue. "I learned it," they answer. My kids learned not to say, and not to think, the "I'll never" phrase; they quickly learned that it's not true and that there's no point in such negative thinking.

As Seligman explains, the same setbacks and tragedies happen to both optimists and pessimists, but optimists weather them better, bouncing back from defeat, while the pessimists give up and become depressed. I'm almost always optimistic. My life has been filled with negative events that seemed major at the time, but that later "worked out for the best." I tend to put a positive spin on "negative" events from my past, like the college experience, which empowers me to find a positive perspective on things as they happen, even if at first they seem like setbacks. I got ripped off when searching for my first apartment in Manhattan, only to end up with a better apartment that I otherwise never would have found. We'll talk about that story and more in Chapter 5, when we discuss being a lifelong learner.

✳ Laugh Up Front

Traveling, while one of life's great pleasures, is often filled with mishaps. Perhaps because we have such high expectations for our vacations, anything less than perfect seems more significant, and is more memorable, than it otherwise would be.

I've already told you the story about my honeymoon and the passports. About 10 years later, the first vacation Marcie and I took after we became parents was a long weekend in Bermuda (Wednesday night to Monday night). On Thursday, we noticed a large poster board on an easel in the hotel lobby. The poster was a map of the Atlantic Ocean, with the southeastern United States, Bermuda, and other resort islands. A spot in the ocean was marked with Thursday's date, indicating the location of a hurricane that was heading straight for Bermuda. The storm was projected to hit us on Monday. On Friday, another spot was marked and the projected path of the storm was revised. This time it was projected to bypass Bermuda. On Saturday, the projected path again had the storm hitting Bermuda on Monday (which it eventually did). We began to look into how we could get out of Bermuda as soon as possible. Neither our airline nor any other could assure us of a Sunday flight. They suggested we come to the airport and wait. On Sunday morning, with the hurricane still projected to hit Bermuda, we headed to the airport. We spent the whole day there until, at 10 pm, we were offered a flight to Philadelphia, which we decided to take, and which brought us into Philly around 1 am The airline paid for us to stay at a local hotel and said they would fly us back to New York the next day. It was the middle of the night and the hotel was disgusting and in a horrible neighborhood. We should have been sleeping comfortably in the Hamilton Princess hotel in Bermuda. Did it mess up our vacation a bit? Sure. But a few days later, comfortably back home, we were telling people the story and laughing about it. And years later it's just an amusing tale about a trip that didn't go quite according to plan.

In October 2000, Marcie and I were in Chicago for a weekend for the wedding of one of our best friends from college. After the Saturday night festivities, we woke up extra early on Sunday morning to take a taxi to the airport. We wanted to get an early start because the Chicago marathon was that morning and we didn't want to get caught up in street closures. We got into the taxi and specifically asked the driver to avoid the marathon route. He said it wasn't starting yet. You know what comes next.

About five minutes into the ride, we got to a red light. Ten police cars came down the cross street. Followed by some runners. Then more. Then more. A sea of runners. There was no way to go forward and no way to back up because the taxi was now boxed in by other cars. We sat tight for a while thinking we could wait it out. But the procession continued. On and on. It was incredible. You've never seen so many people (I later read that there were 33,171 marathoners). We got more and more frustrated as we watched the runners and the minutes pass by. Finally, we paid the driver, got out, and started running in the opposite direction to the subway, carrying our heavy bags (we didn't yet have suitcases with wheels). The subway was slow. Somewhere in the middle of it all, I said to Marcie, "Think of this as an adventure." She said, "You're right, this *is* an adventure." We got to the airport late for our flight, only to find that the plane had been delayed and the passengers had not even boarded yet. Now we have the memory of the adventure, rather than of a ruined day — and rather than the day being forgotten among the many other unmemorable days we all have.

A few years later, we were flying to Florida for a family vacation and had to spend about six hours in the airport because of a hurricane. I told the kids, "This is going to be a great story later, so we might as well enjoy it now, rather than just later." And they did. I've never seen them better behaved.

People always tell these stories. The happy people laugh at their own bad luck, in a good-natured way. So why not laugh up front?

✳ Not Sweating the Small Stuff

When I learned how to drive, my father told me that if I got a speeding ticket, he would take away my driver's license. It didn't matter that the state wouldn't take away my license — he would.

"I don't want to even ask what would happen if I smashed up the car," I replied.

"If it's an accident, if you weren't speeding, nothing," Dad told me.

When he saw my puzzled look, he added, "You can replace a car. You can't replace a person. All that matters is that no one gets hurt."

It wasn't that we had all the money in the world to fix or replace a smashed car — we were financially comfortable, but we weren't wealthy. It wasn't because we had insurance that would pay for the damage (and we definitely had good insurance. Dad was in the insurance business). It was that Dad just didn't care about material things. People mattered. Things didn't. Things were small stuff.

Franklin Delano Roosevelt said something similar. His 1933 inaugural address, most famous for his line, "the only thing we have to fear is fear itself," came as the country was in the depths of the Great Depression.

Things were bad. Everyone knew that. He reminded the country, how-ever, that its difficulties "concern, thank God, only material things."

A few years ago I went to a party at my friend Nick's brand-new office. While preparing hot food, the caterer burned the conference room table. Someone said to Nick, "I can't believe you aren't freaking out." Nick responded, "If I thought getting mad would make it go back to the way it was before, I would." There's so much wisdom in Nick's words. I can't even begin to imagine how many times I have pointlessly expressed my anger about something. If Nick had yelled and screamed, all those nega-tive thoughts would have consumed him and would have ruined the night for him and for others. Instead, he just moved on.

Later, I asked Nick about the table and how he arrived at his philosophy of life. He sounded like my dad when he said, "It's not flesh. That's all that really matters. If you crash a car, if you ruin a table, so what? All that matters is life."

Like my dad, Nick doesn't sweat the small stuff. And it's easy to see why he, like my dad, is a happy person.

For many people, Nick's attitude doesn't come naturally. If that's the case for you, I urge you to read Carlson's *Don't Sweat the Small Stuff*. In fact, no matter who you are or what you are like, Carlson's book is a must-read. It's full of great suggestions for a better, happier life.

In late 2008, as the world economy was collapsing, my sister, Sharon, sent me this e-mail:

> As you know, Jeff [Sharon's husband] came down with pneumonia last Monday. At first, I was totally stressed out. Then sometime last week, I realized: I have no control over events and circumstances, but I *can* control how I feel. So I decided that things could be far

worse, and I have had a newfound positive outlook ever since. This was after I had been feeling very overwhelmed for months, especially recently with the economy, with world events. I realized it's not worth worrying about all of these things — I was making myself crazy. So I'm feeling so much better now, so much more relaxed. Thank goodness, because if it weren't for that, I really would have gone off the deep end when both kids got sick Sunday night, and then I had a car problem — aaahhh. But I laughed.

There is plenty that I like about Sharon's story. And, of course, I like that she got to the point where she laughed. She knew it was going to be a funny story later, so she laughed when it was happening.

I had a bad week (many, in fact) at the end of 2008 as well. Here's what happened one particular week:

On Monday, I received a subpoena to produce a huge amount of paperwork for a lawsuit involving one of our clients. That rarely happens in my business and it was incredibly frustrating because it was going to be costly to comply. On Tuesday, one of our biggest clients announced they were going out of business. On Wednesday, the managing partner of another client, also one of our largest, was arrested for a Madoff-type crime (not billions, only hundreds of millions — oy). His firm owed us hundreds of thousands of dollars at the time. I got very little sleep all week, because I kept waking up in the middle of the night and lying in bed thinking about these crazy things. Then, late Friday, just as I thought the week was mercifully going to end with no more incidents, our company's bookkeeper came to me to ask about a charge on my American Express bill for a stay at the exclusive Plaza Hotel in Manhattan. She didn't have a receipt for the stay and when she called the Plaza to inquire, they confirmed that I had stayed there (I have never stayed there) — and that I was due to check in again that next Monday! This was incredible. What a topper. I started laughing. I thought about all of the week's wacky events and imagined myself recounting them to my friends that weekend. At that moment I realized that pretty soon my crazy week wasn't going to be the calamity it felt like as it was happening, but instead was going to be just an entertaining story. Indeed, by the end of that weekend I had told a bunch of people about my crazy — so crazy it was laughable — week, and that helped me cope with the unfortunate events.

By the way, when I called American Express, they quickly assured me that everything would be resolved. They reversed the charge, canceled my card, and sent me a new one. We later learned that the Plaza situation was a mix-up, not fraud. I have a frequent-stay account with Fairmont, the owner of the Plaza and other hotels. There is more than one David Singer in Fairmont's system, and my account got mixed up with one of the other David Singer accounts. As to the subpoena, it took us many phone calls, some money spent on attorney fees, and many weeks, but we ended up getting out of it. Regarding our client who was arrested and owed us money, we did get paid, he was sentenced to 20 years in jail, and his firm disintegrated, just as the economy tanked and we could least afford to lose one of our largest accounts.

✳ Kevin Teaches Me a Lesson

When my friends Kevin and Megan got married (the Chicago marathon story from above), they had difficulty keeping their guests' attention at the party. Nearly half the guests (most of Kevin's relatives and friends) had flown to Chicago from New York. The problem was that the first game of baseball's 2000 World Series was taking place on the same night as the wedding. And for New Yorkers, this wasn't just any World Series. It was a *Subway Series*, featuring the New York Mets *and* the New York Yankees. Because virtually every New Yorker is either a Mets fan or a Yankees fan, most of the wedding guests from New York had a strong interest in the game. (Ironically, Kevin is not a sports fan.)

At first, the groom was quite dismayed as a crowd gathered around the TV at the restaurant's bar. But when someone suggested that the TV be turned off, Kevin stopped them. "No way," he said. "If you turn it off, they'll all leave and go to a bar down the street." Most important, Kevin decided to focus on the big stuff. He remembered that the most important things were that he and Megan had gotten married that day, and that he was grateful for everyone making the trip halfway across the country for the event. If he got mad, it would just take away from a special moment. He realized that this was simply going to be a funny story in the future, so why not enjoy the humor of the situation as it was happening?

Kevin was following his own advice. I recall the wise words Kevin had spoken to me 16 years earlier, just after college, when he and I had a wonderful opportunity to spend a couple of weeks traveling in Ireland together. Kevin had been working in Ireland as a bartender during the summer. I took an overnight boat from England to Ireland and then a bus across Ireland, meeting up with Kevin in the western part of the country.

He had arranged our travel schedule. The morning after my arrival, we ate breakfast and then put on our backpacks and walked to a bus stop. It was drizzling as we waited. And waited. And waited. Kevin finally admitted that he had simply assumed that a bus was coming and had not checked the schedule. I was flabbergasted. Marcie and I had just traveled around Europe for eight weeks, flawlessly making connections — and never waiting for a bus or train unless we knew the schedule. I whined and complained to Kevin as we continued to wait and wait and wait. Kevin finally said, "What's the point of complaining? It's over. Let's move on and enjoy ourselves." He then told me of a similar situation when he whined during a setback in some travels with his brother and another friend, both of whom told him to knock it off. Looking back, that morning with Kevin is yet another humorous (and instructive) memory.

I can't help but smile when I think back on that story, and all the others. And smiling is a good thing, as we're about to discuss.

✳ Smile and the World Smiles With You

It's true. If you go around with a smile on your face, people will smile back at you. It's so simple, and it makes other people feel good — which, in turn, makes you feel good. Try it.

But it's not just the smiles that come back at you that make you feel good. It's also the act of smiling itself that does the trick. If you smile, you will automatically feel happy. Smile right now. Feel how good you feel. The smile seems to trick the brain into thinking you are happy, which releases the happy chemicals. It's an amazing thing, and simple proof of the mind-body connection.

I'm a big believer in the mind-body connection. I know that the things I think about affect not just my mood, but also how I feel physically. During my freshman year in college, I started getting stomach aches. I went to the infirmary a few times and I took Mylanta, but that didn't help. Then one day something unpleasant happened with my girlfriend and I felt a wave of discomfort descend to my stomach, and soon my stomach started to hurt. From then on, when I felt I was about to get that pain in my stomach, I stopped it by relaxing. I used a form of meditation I learned from my 10th-grade psychology teacher. Mr. Mascari taught us to close our eyes and see the sun, or a light, shining down on the top of our heads. I would feel the warmth as the light crept down my head, over my ears to my neck, over my shoulders, down my chest, my back, and my arms and fingers, down my legs to my feet, and finally enveloped me as it wrapped around my toes. It's a great relaxation exercise.

More recently, I have used breathing techniques that I learned in yoga class. I slowly breathe in through my nose, counting to four, and then exhale from my mouth, counting to eight. In addition to slowing down your breathing (which is often rapid in times of stress), it makes it hard to think about anything else when you are focusing on your breathing. If you are not thinking about anything else, you relax, which is why I also use that breathing technique when I am awake in the middle of the night and want to fall back asleep.

My friend Myra told me the following story about smiles. In 2006, her husband underwent three surgeries and spent months in the hospital. It was an extremely difficult year for Myra, and this is something she wrote about the experience:

> There were weeks when it was touch and go. He had to learn how to eat again, how to walk again. People asked me how I endured, what kept me going. To quote Blanche from *A Streetcar Named Desire*, "I have always depended on the kindness of strangers." On the day of Ed's second surgery, I had bronchitis, was feverish, and felt like I was carrying the weight of the world on my shoulders. Ed lay there unable to talk, so medicated he didn't know I was there. I was doing all I could to save him and yet knew he could die at any minute. I slept with the lights on and two phones at hand so I could speak to doctors at 2 am if they called.

> My friends were amazing, but when I looked into their eyes I saw the pain I was carrying mirrored back at me. I needed the warmth of strangers, people who didn't know my situation to give me the fuel to endure. The smile I got each night from the man at the hospital garage was my good night. It was the last warm human face I would see till I got to work in the morning. I cherished that and got into the habit of always going to the same person because he was the warmest one at the gate. I lingered over it the way you savor that relaxing cup of coffee after a fine meal.

I started seeking out smiles. Chit-chatting with people in the elevator, helping others in distress. I would say hello and smile at every patient I saw, do all I could to make them feel warm and cared for. I was addicted to smiles. I wanted to hug the world and say, "It is okay, we will endure whatever you're going through together." I needed people to smile at me to remind me I was alive and a human. In those smiles I saw hope.

Smiles will make any pain easier to endure; they will lift you up in your darkest hour. They contain a power so great, they can turn your existence completely around. They can give you warmth so intense that the coldest heart will melt. When you're in pain, give them to strangers; the joy you will receive from them in return will help you feel that you're gaining a foothold when life is spinning out of control.

Smiling and being happy — they're connected at the hip, or, more accurately, connected at the lip.

✳ How Ya Doin'? Great!

Another way to trick your brain is with your response to the simple question, "How are you?" Most of us say, "Okay" or "Fine" or "Good" or "Not bad" or "Busy" when we are asked that question. Instead, get into the habit of saying, "Great!" or "Excellent!" When you say great, you'll start to feel great because repeatedly engaging in a behavior can bring about internal change, even if you are just going through the motions. And besides, if you say that things are great, you'll be telling the truth. After all, things *are* great — you're alive, aren't you? Even during the times when we feel that most things are working against us — a heavy workload at the office, money problems, family issues — we have so much to be grateful for. During the stock market "crash" of 2008, there was so much misery, so many people worrying about their 401(k) plans and their other savings. The happiest people were the ones who were appreciating what was around them and all they had to be grateful for — their families, their health, even the flowers and the trees.

One day in November 2008, my wife and I walked by a guy coming out of his house. We were a few blocks from our house, but we didn't know him. He asked, in a neighborly way, "How ya doin?" and I said, "Excellent." I think that took him by surprise. He chuckled and said, "You don't hear that too often." It's true. And not only should you do this, but you shouldn't stand for others saying anything less. Challenge them. When they say, "Okay," say, "Only okay?" Or if they say, "Not bad," challenge them. "Why 'not bad'? That's so negative. How about good?" Get them to say they are doing well. Same thing when they utter that other common line, "Hangin' in there." It's amazing how easily we accept mediocre life as normal and acceptable. And it's amazing how high we can all rise above "hangin' in there" and "not bad" just by using more positive language.

Another of my least favorite responses is "Busy." "Busy" almost always comes across as a negative response; a complaint. But that changed when the economic downturn began in late 2008. As people lost their jobs in droves, "busy" was no longer a complaint, but rather something those without jobs wished they could say. Situations like those help us to appreciate what we have. Being busy is something to be thankful for, something we should choose to be happy about, as so many of us learned during the financial crisis.

In the same way as that guy who Marcie and I passed was surprised by my response, I was surprised by two great replies I received soon after that. One was from my neighbor Hal. He had come over to my house to help me with something. As he was leaving, I thanked him and said, "Have a great day." He looked at me and answered, "I always do." I love that. Hal *does* always have great days. When I first met him, he had a dog named Lucky — so named because Hal felt so lucky, so blessed, with everything he had been given in this world. The other surprise answer I got was on a phone call to the burglar alarm company. I needed a service call at our house. As the call ended, the representative said, "Have a nice day." I said, "Thank you. You too." She said, "I will." You don't hear that a lot and I loved it. She sounded like a happy person. And she sounded like someone who loves her job — which is the subject of the next section.

✳ You Have to Love What You Do

In 1985, the year after I graduated from college, I was working at my first job, as a "consultant" for a large company that I will call "the firm." The firm had three divisions at that time and I was in the consulting division. I hated my time there. I lasted nine months. (I have to add here that, looking back now, more than 25 years later, the whole experience is another funny and instructive story.)

I had first heard of the firm when they came to my campus, the State University of New York (SUNY) at Albany, to recruit business majors. I had done very well in college and was offered the job — an offer others coveted. In fact, the job was considered so desirable that I accepted it even though I had another offer for more money.

My career at the firm began with a six-week training program. After the training, my first assignment went well. The project manager wrote a favorable memo for my file: "David is an independent worker who demonstrated a good ability to identify problems and develop practical, workable solutions. He manages his time well and worked additional hours as he felt appropriate, in order to complete his assignments on-time." That first assignment was considered a short one — it lasted less than three weeks. It was interesting, and it was challenging. I learned new things, and I enjoyed it. Unfortunately, that was my last good assignment.

My second project manager had this to say: "Overall, David's performance was highly satisfactory... David is intelligent, picks up quickly on new concepts, and always completes assignments given to him." Sounds pretty good. However, it continued, "David must learn to cooperate without hesitation, and develop enthusiasm and motivation for his work."

What happened? On this project I was regularly assigned to photocopying, binding (putting computer printouts into binders), and dittoing (making copies of computer tapes). I was bored. I felt that my talent and abilities were being wasted. After all, the firm had come to my college to recruit me, I had received a rating of "outstanding" in the firm's six-week training program, and I had performed very well on my first assignment.

Then I did the unthinkable — I complained to my manager. He yelled at me and said, "Accept your shit work." Very inspirational. So I spoke with his manager. "Stick with it" were his words of wisdom.

I told my dad about my predicament. He said, "Go to the top — speak with the guy who runs the company." I tried to get to the firm's managing partner, but I couldn't. I tried to get to the level right below the managing partner, the head of the consulting division, but I couldn't get to him, either.

There were three divisions within consulting and I succeeded in getting a meeting with the head of my division. That was pretty high up. It was the third level of the company (which had about 24,000 employees), and it was three levels higher than my manager's manager.

I met with Mr. Big. He had a huge, beautiful office. I told him about my disappointing experience. He listened attentively, and then said, "Look. Even in my job I have a lot of shit work. Probably 50 percent of what I do, I don't like. But it's that other 50 percent that makes it worthwhile."

That evening I told my dad. He was astounded. "You're telling me that this guy, the guy who is five levels above you, the guy with the job that you hope to someday get to if you work in his company for many, many years, that guy thinks it's inspiring to tell you that *50 percent* of the time he doesn't like his job? I like my job *99 percent* of the time. In fact, I *love* my job. You've got to get out of there."

Until then, no one had told me that I had to love my job.

✳ You Have to Do What You Love

One of my favorite examples of someone doing what he loves is a guy named Lawrence who went to my high school. Lawrence and I were not at school together, because he's eight years younger than I am. I graduated with Lawrence's brother, who was the starting point guard on the school's basketball team, which almost won the state championship. A couple of years later, Lawrence's next brother was the starting point guard on the team. But Lawrence didn't make the team, although he loved playing basketball. He also loved coaching basketball — starting with a penchant for diagramming plays for driveway games with his older brothers and neighborhood friends, and continuing with a gig he got as a player-coach in a youth league. One summer, Lawrence wanted to attend the famous Five-Star basketball camp, to learn how to coach. They told him something to the effect of, "You don't understand, our camp is for players, not aspiring coaches." He wrote them a letter saying that he understood that, but that he wanted to come and learn how to coach. He persuaded them to give him a job doing other things at the camp. Then, whenever he had a break, he stood on the court, clipboard in hand, next to the coaches, watching and learning.

Lawrence went to Indiana University. I have no idea what his major was or what he wanted to learn in his classes. He went to Indiana, he has said, because of its legendary basketball coach, Bob Knight. He spent four years at Indiana as the basketball manager, doing whatever Coach Knight asked him to do, including cleaning the floors of the gym. Then, in 2004, at age 33, Lawrence Frank became the head coach of the New Jersey Nets. That's incredibly young to become an NBA head coach. "I know it sounds corny," he has said, "but when you love what you do, and it's a passion, it's not a job."

Few people know what they want to do as early as Lawrence Frank did, which is one reason why my favorite approach to helping you do what you love is Dan Sullivan's *Unique Ability*® concept. Dan (to whom I have become quite close since we first met in 1994) is the co-founder of the Strategic Coach® Program I mentioned in this book's introduction, which I strongly recommend for entrepreneurs. His approach helps you figure out your true calling — the activities that you should be spending most of your time doing. (Check out *Unique Ability*®: *Creating the Life You Want* at StrategicCoach.com.)

When I have run workshops for high school students about this subject, I tell them that I understand it's hard for them to already know what they want to do for the rest of their lives. If they know, great — but if they don't, that's fine. I don't ask them to decide their career paths. What I *do* want them to decide is that they will spend their lives doing things they love to do — whatever those things might be.

✳ You Can Do Anything if You Put Your Team's Mind to It

One potential problem with trying to focus all your time on the things you are best at, and love to do, is that there are other things we have to do that we are not good at, and don't enjoy doing. The easiest solution is to spend money to have someone else do those things for you. The return you will get on that investment is huge. Notice that I called it an investment, not a cost. By investing in having others do those things, you'll have more time to spend on the things you should be focusing on, and as a result, you'll make more money. In fact, you'll make so much more money that you'll be able to afford doing even more things you love to do — hobbies, vacations, and spending time with your family and friends.

In a successful business, it's pretty easy to see this in action. For example, in my office some people love selling, others love providing customer service, others love answering the phone, others love bookkeeping, etc. The more people we have performing roles they love, the more likely it is that our business will prosper.

When I speak with high school students I usually ask them to raise their hands if they've heard the saying, "You can do anything if you put your mind to it." Almost all of them raise their hands. I then ask for another show of hands: "Who believes that?" Again, nearly all of them raise their hands. (I don't know whether they really believe it or whether they assume that's what I want to hear.) So far, they probably think they know exactly where I'm headed. But they're almost always surprised by what comes next. "I'm not 100 percent sure I believe it," I tell them, and that usually gets their attention. I then explain: "Here's what I *do* believe. When you are doing things you love to do, *then* you can do anything, if you put your mind to it." And if you're operating in areas that require a combination of different activities, the key is to find others who love the activities that you don't enjoy. Then, as a team, you really *can* do anything.

Think about a basketball team. If all five players are really good at offense, but none can play defense, they'll score a lot but they won't win. If they all play great defense, but nobody can score, they will play a lot of low-scoring games, but they won't win. The secret to a winning basketball team is to have five people who work together to provide great scoring, great defense, great rebounding, and great passing.

This often-told story nicely captures the importance of the team approach:

> One day a small boy tried to lift a heavy stone but couldn't budge it. His father, watching, finally said, "Are you sure you're using all your strength?"
>
> "Yes," the boy replied.
>
> "No, you're not," said the father. "You haven't asked me to help you."

✳ Bartering

When we talk about investing in others to do things that we're not passionate about doing ourselves, what usually comes to mind is spending money to hire those people. But what if you don't have the money to make that investment? Try bartering. For example, Marcie (my wife) is extremely organized and she helped my sister-in-law, Michey, organize her house. In exchange, Michey has helped Marcie to shop for clothes for our daughters — something that Michey loves to do, but that Marcie finds frustrating. Meanwhile, after Marcie helped Michey and several other friends get more organized, she realized how much she loves doing that — so she became a professional organizer.

Michey and her husband (my brother), Jon, have a daughter with autism. Jon wrote a wonderful book for families with kids who have special needs, *The Special Needs Parent Handbook*. From his book:

> One thing that is very important in our relationships with our "family circle," especially with my brother and his family, is that we are able to barter in ways we can help each other. Your goal

should be to try to make the relationship mutually beneficial. For example, there have been times that we have helped watch their kids so they could take vacations alone together, and my wife takes their kids shopping.

Within our house, Marcie and I barter: I write holiday cards after Marcie picks out the photo and the card. Marcie buys all the gifts for birthdays and events we are invited to — she's very organized and has amazing ideas. I fill out all forms, such as for the kids' sports and school programs. I take out the trash and recycling on the appropriate days, while Marcie does the laundry, though that's partly because she says that I ruined some of her and the kids' clothing by not knowing what I was doing — oops.

Some people avoid bartering because they think it will make them seem, or feel, less capable. So many of us feel we have to be good at everything — or at least at all of those things that fall into our "assigned role" in life. For example, a stay-at-home mom might feel that she has to be a good cook. Yet, not everyone can be a good cook. This is important: There is *no reason* to be ashamed about not being good at certain things. None of us is good at everything — it's just not possible. We will all experience failure at certain things we try, and that's okay.

The flip side is that we're all good at certain things. Howard Gardner and Joseph Walters, authors of the well-respected theory of "multiple intelligences," identify at least seven types of intelligence: musical, bodily-kinesthetic (like Michael Jordan's basketball-playing intelligence), logical-mathematical (doing well on the math SAT), linguistic (doing well on the reading SAT), spatial (a trip navigator exhibits this), interpersonal (ability to communicate with others), and intrapersonal (knowledge of the internal aspects of yourself). Gardner and Walters explain that we all have some intelligence in each of these areas, and certain people have an extremely high level of intelligence in a particular area.

Tony Hsieh (pronounced "Shay"), CEO of the online shoe seller Zappos.com (acquired in 2009 by Amazon.com), was asked in a May 2009 interview in *Inc.* magazine to name the smartest person he knew. He replied that people are smart in different ways and that with everyone he meets, he tries to figure out what they're smart about and learn from them — which is a clear, simple illustration of the idea of multiple intelligences.

In the same way that we are all good at certain things, we all have things we are not good at. And that's okay. Max De Pree, former CEO of furniture maker Herman Miller, explains in his fine book *Leadership is an Art* that we should admit we can't do everything and we should rely on others' strengths to pick up the slack.

It was hard for my wife to embrace the idea that it's okay to not be great at everything. Marcie had an ideal picture of herself that included, among other things, being an ideal mother, being a great cook, and being a terrific shopper. While she was competent at these tasks, she was destined to be a failure in her own mind because she was unable to reach the ideal.

Everyone will tell you that Marcie is a wonderful mother. She's warm, nurturing, and loving. She thinks about her kids all the time and would do anything for them. She loves her children and loves being their mom, but Marcie doesn't enjoy some of the tasks of being "mom." She hates getting the kids to do their homework, making their meals only to have them say, "I don't want chicken," telling them when to go to bed, etc. She used to see these as shortcomings, which caused her anxiety.

We got over some of these issues by hiring people to help us with those particular tasks. For example, the homework part was solved when we realized we could hire high school students to do what Marcie had been doing — not to be tutors, but to sit with our kids occasionally to make sure they were on track. Our first "homework helper" was a senior in high school, the older sister of one of our son's friends. At the end of that school year, she referred us to a junior who could be the following year's helper. We've been able to do the same thing every year since.

When my son was a junior in high school, he was hired as a homework helper for other families. One day at the supermarket I ran into a mom who had hired him and I asked her how it was working out. "I don't have to do homework anymore," she told me with glee. "My son responds so much better to your son than he does to me. He's a good role model. And I don't get aggravated. It's wonderful."

It's okay to love being the mother of your children but to hate doing the mom job. Get help. Find others who love doing the things that you don't enjoy. Hiring people to do the "home" tasks that you hate pays huge dividends in your quality of life. That's why so many people hire people to help them clean, do laundry, and even cook. Having a cook sounds like something only for the rich and famous, but my wife discovered that many of the people who have done cleaning for us are also very good at cooking — or even just food prep. For example, Marcie has them cut up several days' worth of vegetables for us to serve the kids after school.

✳ Don't Try This at Home

The *New York Times* ran a front-page feature article in May 2009 called "Even if You Want to Save Cash, Don't Try This Stuff at Home." It was about people who, because of the difficult economy, decided to "do-it-yourself" rather than hiring a handyman or other professional, only to find that it cost much more in the long run due to mistakes they made. One woman, who decided to replace a toilet herself, was happy until the ceiling collapsed in the room below the toilet. Then, as she rushed out to get supplies to repair the leak, she hit a pole in her garage, ripping the bumper off her car and causing several shelves holding flowerpots and garden tools to collapse. In the end, she called a handyman.

She lost time, she undoubtedly experienced a great deal of stress, and in the end it cost her more money. Her story demonstrates why hiring others to do what you are not great at is a good investment, not a cost to be avoided.

✳ You Can Even Barter at Work

Bartering can even work at your place of employment. There are people you work with who love doing aspects of your job that you hate. In exchange, you can do things that they hate to do.

In an interview in *Selling Power* magazine, Marcus Buckingham, author of *Now, Discover Your Strengths*, suggested partnering with colleagues to avoid doing the things you don't like to do. He gave an example familiar to the salespeople in my company when he suggested that those who love cold calling should partner with those who love to maintain accounts. He went so far as to say that it's a waste of time to try to master every aspect of a given task when you and a partner can handle it in a more productive and enjoyable way by each focusing on the parts that you love to do.

✳ The 80/20 Rule

I first heard of the 80/20 rule, also known as the Pareto Principle (because of its discovery in 1897 by Italian economist Vilfredo Pareto), while watching a video in the mid-'90s called *Forcing Vertical Growth*, by Roger Sitkins, an insurance agency consultant. Sitkins explained that one of the ways to make our business more successful would be to identify the 20 percent of our clients who produce 80 percent of our revenues, and then to allocate the appropriate time and resources that those top 20 percent merit. He instructed us to make a list of our clients from largest to smallest, in terms of revenue to us, and predicted that the top 20 percent in terms of size would account for 80 percent of our total revenues. We did the analysis and found that he was exactly right.

A few years later, Richard Koch wrote a very good book called *The 80/20 Principle*. Koch explains that the 80/20 principle should lead us to be selective, to strive to be top performers in the few things we love to do, instead of trying to be adequate at everything. He says we should delegate as much as possible to specialists (gardeners, mechanics, decorators, etc.), while focusing on things we excel at and love to do. Think about it this way: If you are currently spending only 20 percent of your time doing what you are great at and love to do, and that 20 percent creates 80 percent of your results, imagine if you could spend 40 percent of your time on those things. You should see your results double. Even if your results don't quite double, they will certainly improve significantly. Then you can use the extra money you earn to hire more people for the other things you need done. The result: the Holy Grail of accomplishing more in less time. As my dad told me many times when I was young, "Work smarter, not harder."

✳ Delegation is Not Dumping

Hiring others to do things you don't like to do or are not good at, at home or at work, does not mean you are *dumping* those undesirable tasks on someone else. My company's longtime chief operating officer, Mark Shanock, who is a close friend of mine, addressed this issue in the following memo:

> Delegation is a common business term whose meaning has mutated and degenerated over the years. Upon hearing or using the word, people falsely believe it means to pass off

responsibility, or worse, to push down a necessary task that is not "worth their time."

The true meaning of Delegate (from the dictionary) is: to entrust to another. This is exactly what we are trying to achieve on a daily basis within our own company. Delegation is a distinguished and valuable tool that this organization uses to maximize the potential of every individual.

Each of us has a well-defined role that contributes to our success. I am certain that none of us would want to delegate the role of sales to me. As an organization we have delegated that to our salespeople. We have entrusted our salespeople to generate the income that we all rely upon. The firm has also entrusted our Account Representatives to meet the daily service needs of our clients and the Admin staff to handle many of our daily support needs.

We are an organization made up of individuals who do not dump or neglect our responsibilities. There is no such thing as delegating up or down. Each of us has our unique abilities and roles that are critical to our success. Skills change and improve. Just as we work on changing and improving what we do and how we operate as a company, our individual roles will constantly be redefined and developed. Delegation is a conduit for continuing that professional development.

Understanding the accurate definition of the word Delegate and how important each individual is to our success will make our organization truly special.

The fact that we're all different helps us make progress and accomplish things. If everyone brought the same skills to the table, not a lot would get done. As I like to say, "I'm not better than you and you're not better than me. But I *am* better than you at *certain things*, and you're better than me at certain things." The fact that someone spends their time doing things you don't like to do doesn't mean that they're doing demeaning things. It doesn't mean they aren't doing something that is their calling or life's purpose. Po Bronson, author of *What Should I Do With My Life?*, explains that work provides a sense of purpose when you love what you do *and* you also get a wonderful feeling of accomplishment from it. For example, hotelier Chip Conley, the founder and CEO of Joie de Vivre Hospitality, explains in his book *Peak* that among the people he hires to clean hotel rooms, the ones who are most successful are passionate about creating pleasant experiences for guests who use the rooms.

Jonathan Haidt provides a similar example in his well-researched book, *The Happiness Hypothesis*. He cites a study by Amy Wrzesniewski, a psychologist at New York University, which found that hospital janitors who saw their job as a calling, who considered themselves part of a healing team, would go over and above their normal job requirements — by trying to brighten up the rooms of very sick patients, for instance, or by anticipating the needs of doctors and nurses rather than waiting for orders. The janitors who worked this way, Haidt writes, "enjoyed it far more than those who saw it as a job."

Haidt echoes so many others we have discussed when he recommends knowing your strengths and choosing work that allows you to focus on those strengths. It also sounds familiar when he explains that you don't have to know how to do everything. You should either figure out how you can accomplish a task by using your strengths, or you should delegate the task to someone who excels at whatever skills are needed.

Haidt says that you should work on your strengths, not your weaknesses, and Dan Sullivan makes a similar point. So many people talk about working hard to improve their weaknesses, but Dan says that if you do that you'll end up with lots of strong weaknesses. ☺

✳ I Repeat, You Have to Do What You Love

Even though it seems obvious that people will be more successful and happier if they spend their lives doing things that they enjoy, we all know people (probably many of them) who complain that they don't like their job.

Because you're going to go through your life doing something, it might as well be something that you enjoy.

Steven Jobs, the founder and CEO of Apple, made a similar point in his June 2005 commencement speech at Stanford: "You've got to find what you love. And that is as true for your work as it is for your lovers. Your work going to fill a large part of your life, and the only way to be truly satisfied is to do what you believe is great work. And the only way to do great work is to love what you do. If you haven't found it yet, keep looking. Don't settle."

✳ Don't Wish Away Your Activities and Forget to Live

In the next chapter I talk about how being present with other people — giving them your full and undivided attention — is an important component to being nice. Being present is also an important tool to help you to be happy.

When people don't enjoy their life's activities, they wish them away. For example, if they don't like parenting young children, they wish their kids were older. Then, when their kids get older, those same people wish the kids were young again.

A friend forwarded this e-mail to me:

> First I was dying to finish my high school and start college.
> And then I was dying to finish college and start working.
> Then I was dying to marry and have children.

> And then I was dying for my children to grow old enough so I
> could go back to work.
> But then I was dying to retire.
> And now I'm dying.
> And suddenly I realized I forgot to live.

When my oldest child began the process of applying to college, many
friends asked me, "Can you believe that so many years have passed? Isn't
it amazing how the years fly by?" My answer was, "Yes, I *can* believe it."
As I explained to them, while I certainly looked back with amazement at
how fast the time flew by, I also had experienced a very rich, rewarding
and eventful 18 years as a dad; so it made sense that my kid was getting
ready to go to college. Being very involved in my kids' lives and "being
present" was a great gift that I gave to my kids and to myself.

Marcie and I tried to enjoy all of our parenting duties, including those
that might seem like a drag. For example, we like staying up until midnight on New Year's Eve, but when our kids were young we knew that
if we did we would pay the price when they woke us up at 6 am. So we
went to bed before the ball dropped. That was definitely a *life is long*
moment for us. We knew we would have many more years of staying
up until midnight on New Year's Eve, so we gave up that pleasure and
embraced what we had to do at that moment in our lives. And it made
us happy. When it came to changing diapers — a parenting task that
many people wish away — maybe I was a little bit lucky; I didn't love
it, but I didn't hate it, either. And my competitive nature helped me
make it a point of pride to do it as fast as possible. I got really good at
it — changing thousands of diapers in a two-year period will give you
that opportunity. I can go on and on, naming "sacrifices" we made and
recounting moments that we might have wished away but that we instead decided to be present for and enjoy for what they were.

I also acknowledged that *life is long* when I decided to attend as many of my kids' music concerts, soccer games, tae kwon do tests, and other events as I possibly could. I knew that I would always look back on those times with fondness, and that there would be plenty of years later on to have a single-minded focus on work if that's what I wanted. I also learned that the peace of mind and enjoyment I got from being a "present" dad made me more content in general, which would help me to be more successful at everything I did, including my job, so there would be a net gain overall.

✳ Gratitude, Another Bit of Magic

The importance of gratitude, of saying thank you, is usually discussed in the context of our interactions with other people, but gratitude is also a critical part of being happy. It's hard to be unhappy when you are grateful. Numerous studies have shown that keeping a journal of things you feel grateful for helps you to be happier. People tend to ruminate on negative things at the end of each day. To counteract that tendency, at the end of each day make a list of things for which you are grateful. If you feel you had a "bad day" and don't know where to begin your gratitude, don't think about things specifically from that day. Think about the trees. Aren't you grateful for them? Think about the human brain. Aren't you grateful for your brain? Think about the medical advances that will enable you to live longer. Think about music. I am constantly grateful for music. I am also grateful for sports, humor, books, movies, and of course my family and friends.

Thanksgiving is a holiday on which we are taught to be grateful, to give thanks. In 2008, as the economic crisis was unfolding, I received a wonderful Thanksgiving greeting from a company that polled its employees on what they were thankful for, and shared a compilation of responses:

For my family and for their health; For having such a wonderful family, good health and children that are independent, loving and self sufficient; For my health and the health of my family and friends. I'm also incredibly grateful for the important people in my life and all the support they provide me. You could have all the material possessions in the world, but without your health and supportive relationships you'd really be very poor; For my family and friends, my good health, and my sense of humor; That I am here, healthy, and able to enjoy every day of my life; For my family, for a warm bed at night, and hot showers in the morning; For having great kids, health, and the ability to have a good time. I love nothing more than celebrating happy occasions with family and friends; For a supportive family, a great bunch of friends.

That paragraph is worth rereading if you're feeling down from a bad day or an upsetting experience.

I personally know some of Bernie Madoff's victims, including Burt Ross, the landlord of the office building where my company is located. He lost more than $5 million in the Madoff scheme, but his perspective on it has been inspirational. "He hasn't ruined my life," Ross said of Madoff in a newspaper interview. "I wake up in the morning. My wife who I adore is on my pillow. I have kids I adore. I have a network of friends. I'm not a victim, I'm a survivor."

✳ Larger Than Yourself

Happiness is about so much more than the size of your bank account. In October 2008, at the height of the financial crisis, Nicholas Kristof of the *New York Times* wrote a column about some potential upsides of the economic downturn and he noted that happiness is more about friendships and "finding meaning in a cause larger than oneself" than about money. Kristof went on to quote Alan Krueger, a Princeton University economist who has conducted extensive research on happiness. "There's pretty good evidence that money doesn't matter much for how you feel moment to moment," Krueger said. "What seems to matter much more is having good friends and family, and time to spend on social activities."

"Finding meaning in a cause larger than oneself" is a common theme in a lot of inspirational reading. As Norman Vincent Peale tells us in *The Power of Positive Thinking*, "The more you lose yourself in something bigger than yourself, the more energy you will have. You won't have time to think about yourself and get bogged down in your emotional difficulties."

One of the best writers on the subject of finding meaning in a cause larger than yourself is Viktor Frankl, whose father, mother, brother, and wife died in Nazi concentration camps. In *Man's Search for Meaning*, published in 1946, Frankl describes his experiences as a concentration camp prisoner and how he found a reason to keep living. The book was a major inspiration for Stephen Covey and many other personal-development gurus.

Frankl says that happiness is a side effect of personal dedication to a cause greater than yourself. He cites as inspiration a quote from the 19th-century German philosopher Friedrich Nietzsche: "He who has a *why* to live can bear with almost any *how*." Rather than thinking about his day-to-day existence while he was a prisoner in the concentration camp, Frankl saw a picture of himself in the future, lecturing on the psychology of the concentration camp. He even began thinking of his ongoing sufferings as if they were in the past. (This is the ultimate version of "since it's going to be a story later, start thinking about the story now.")

✳ Perfectionism Makes it Hard to Be Happy

I mentioned in the introduction that I know I'm not perfect. Sometimes I worry, though, that my standards are too high. It was with that in mind that I decided to read *Never Good Enough: How to Use Perfectionism to Your Advantage Without Letting it Ruin Your Life,* by Monica Ramirez Basco. Basco explains that outwardly focused perfectionists experience problems in their relationships because they are frequently frustrated by other people's failures to meet their expectations. When I read her book, Basco joined the ranks of amazing authors who have bowled me over by writing something that felt like it was essentially all about me. It hit home for me when she talked about perfectionists being rigid in their views and it helped me tremendously in my relationships with my family members when I realized that while my way was the right way for me, it wasn't the right way for everyone.

I became much happier, as did my family, when I stopped being disappointed when others didn't do things the way I assumed was "right" — the way I assumed everyone knew and agreed was "right." I gradually learned to ease up on what had become criticism of people around me, and my frustration dissipated as I stopped sweating what in most cases was very, very small stuff.

Basco also includes a chapter to share with your family, to help them to have the proper expectations about your perfectionism. Sharing information with others about behaviors of yours that might cause stress for them (and therefore for you) is a great idea. My wife, Marcie, fortunately is already familiar with my behaviors after many years of studying me. She knows how I am about certain things and compensates for my sensitivities. In Chapter 4, I'm going to talk about being organized, something that has served me well, and that will serve you well. That said, I can be extreme in my desire to be organized, feeling strongly, for example, about having "a place for everything, and everything in its place." To compensate, Marcie has always been sure to let me know when household work might disrupt my things. Borrowing from the title of Dr. Spencer Johnson's famous book about dealing with change, *Who Moved*

My Cheese?, she might say to me in the morning, "By the way, a painter is coming today, so when you get home you'll probably find that someone has moved your cheese." Marcie's awareness of how I am, and her communication around that knowledge, has been incredibly helpful for both of us.

✳ The Expectations Gap

Your happiness can so often be impacted by your expectations. If someone calls you and says they are running late, you might not be happy, but you'll probably be more unhappy if they don't call, and you'll grow angrier and angrier as it gets later and later.

When Marcie was pregnant for the first time we were given the book, *What to Expect When You're Expecting*. I loved that book because it helped prepare us for what was to come. I also loved our Lamaze classes. Actually I found the classes boring, but when it came to the delivery room, it was fantastic that we had taken them. The Lamaze breathing unfortunately did little to help Marcie's pain, but what we learned in the classes helped prepare us for the childbirth experience. Becoming a parent is such a wonderful thing, but childbirth is a medical procedure, and things can go wrong. If we had known nothing about childbirth, we would have been concerned when the doctor said, "You're not dilating enough, we had better give you Pitocin." Instead, we said, "Oh, Pitocin, of course."

The same thing happened when my daughter was 15 and tore the ACL (anterior cruciate ligament) in her left leg playing high school soccer. Although virtually every expert recommends surgery for people with this injury — especially teens — who want to play sports again, and the procedure is relatively common, surgery is something my wife and I have never taken lightly, especially for our kids. The injury occurred on a Monday and an ER doctor told us Monday night that there were no broken bones. The next day an orthopedist told us that it was almost certainly a torn ACL, which an MRI confirmed. By the time we met with an orthopedic surgeon on Friday, we had read up on ACL reconstruction surgery on the Internet, spoken with several parents of teens who had gone through the same surgery, and consulted with my cousin, who had trained in orthopedics. As a result, when the surgeon spelled out his recommendations for us, and explained what to expect, there was little we were hearing for the first time, which made the experience much easier, much less scary, and much more beneficial for all of us.

Richard Carlson talks a lot about expectations in *Don't Sweat the Small Stuff With Your Family*. He advises you, for example, to expect that kids will bicker and complain, and that your house will always need upkeep and repair, and he provides many great suggestions to help you understand and accept that such things are a normal part of daily life. I remember when Marcie once said to the kids during dinner, "I'm sick of this. You kids just keep complaining." My daughter Julie, only 6 years old at the time, said, "But you keep complaining about us complaining."

✳ Predictable, Sleepless Nights

The first time I remember having sleepless nights was in 1994. My company was involved in a lawsuit. We had gone through the breakup of a business relationship and had sued the other side, which had violated the terms of our agreement. The case went to arbitrators, as called for in our agreement. At each arbitration session, we had to listen to the other side's version of events. And each night after the sessions I would wake up at 2 am or 3 am. I would lie in bed, unable to fall back asleep as I thought about how to prove our case. I would get out of bed and write down my ideas to use the next time we met with the arbitrators, and then with that off my mind I was able to fall back asleep.

I was unhappy about the lost sleep, but as the arbitration proceedings and lost sleep continued, I began to embrace what was happening. I realized that those middle-of-the-night moments of quiet solitude were helping me to solve my problems. And if I was tired the next day, I would catch up on the sleep within a few days. Despite the lost sleep, I made sure to keep waking up at my normal time so I would have enough time for exercise, which helped keep my energy level up. Since that time, I've maintained a more positive approach to those late-night strategy sessions with myself. I would still rather not wake up in the middle of the night, but I accept it, and I make it work for me. The middle of the night is a bit like being in the shower or driving alone. Many of my best thoughts come to me in those places of solitude.

Prevention.com lists an overactive mind as the primary reason why we stay awake in the middle of the night. They quote Colleen E. Carney, an assistant professor of psychiatry at the Insomnia and Sleep Research Program at Duke University Medical Center, as saying, "People have little control over their thoughts, because they may be going in and out of a light stage of sleep, even though they think they're awake." Tell me about it! If lack of sleep becomes too much of a problem for you, they suggest that you go to another part of the house. Another of their suggestions that has been helpful to me is to write down my pressing concerns, along with possible solutions, a few hours before going to bed. This way I get the issues down on paper and don't ruminate about them if I wake up in the middle of the night.

✳ Anxiety Over Uncertainty is Normal

When I can't sleep at night it's almost always because I am thinking about something that is uncertain. Knowing that it's normal to be kept awake by those situations helps me feel better about the lost sleep, and also about the situations.

As a general rule, people don't like uncertainty. My friend Gary said to me recently, "You know when someone says 'I've got good news and bad news'? I always ask for the bad news first, so it's not lingering."

In a piece in the *New York Times* during the 2009 recession, Daniel Gilbert, professor of psychology at Harvard University and author of a book I very much enjoyed, *Stumbling on Happiness*, cited studies that explained that people feel worse when something bad *might* happen than when something bad *will* happen. He explains that bad news is upsetting, but we quickly work to put it behind us, whereas uncertainty is harder to manage.

But we can also overcome the fear of uncertainty by adjusting our perspective. The Dalai Lama says in *Ethics for the New Millennium* that when we know how to solve a problem, we don't need to be anxious about it, we just need to focus our energies on the solution; and when we don't know how to solve a problem, worrying about it won't help, so don't do it.

In *Feel the Fear and Do It Anyway,* author Susan Jeffers, PhD, says that the problem is in our heads. More than 90 percent of what we worry about never happens, Jeffers writes, so if we worry all the time, we are not being realistic. As Mark Twain famously wrote, "I have been through some terrible things in my life, some of which actually happened."

✳ optimismisgood

Martin Seligman (author of *Learned Optimism*) and his group at the University of Pennsylvania advise people to write down three good things that happen each day. This makes you pay more attention to those good things, which might otherwise be overlooked, and stops you from focusing only on the day's disappointments. I'm a naturally optimistic person, but I learned from Dan Sullivan the importance of instilling optimism in your children by teaching them the habit of thinking about their achievements at the end of each day. On Dan's advice, I started doing that on a nightly basis with my son, Jeremy, when he was 7. Some of the achievements from his first few weeks were: I got my black stripe in tae kwon do; I got everything right in phonics; the piano teacher said I improved; I got everything right on my spelling test; I was louder than a brown belt in tae kwon do; I was behaving better in school; I put a Lego together by myself.

One has to imagine that this had a positive impact on Jeremy. It certainly can't have been bad to review those achievements with him at the end of each day. What I can report is that a few years later, when he was still quite young and was deciding on a screen name for his instant messenger account, Jeremy chose "optimismisgood." I knew he was a positive kid. I knew he had achieved a lot (by then he had become a black belt in tae kwon do, had given up piano and taken up drums, and had maintained good grades in school). But I had no idea he even knew what the word optimism was, let alone that he would choose optimismisgood as his screen name. Pretty cool.

✳ Be Happy

In *The Happiness Hypothesis*, Jonathan Haidt explains that genetics impact our happiness. Meaning, some people are more predisposed to be happy, are more naturally happy, than others. All the more reason to work on your happiness. All the more reason to ask yourself every day, am I happy? And, if not, please use some of the ideas in this chapter to improve your happiness. The name of this chapter is *Be Happy*. I want you to *choose* happiness. I am telling you to take charge of your happiness. Take the name of the chapter as an order from me, to you, to be happy. You have to agree, it's much better than the alternative. ☺

✳ New Habits and Progress

Remember: *Life is long*, meaning we have time. If we try to make a million changes all at once, we often end up so overwhelmed that we make none. Instead, if we *slow down to make the changes*, and then *stop to celebrate the progress*, we'll accomplish much more.

Slow Down to Make the Changes — It takes 21 days to form a new habit. What are some ideas you have for new habits you would like to adopt following your reading of Chapter 1?

Stop to Celebrate the Progress — Remember to look back on all that you've accomplished. What are some areas of progress you've made?

Chapter 2
Be Nice

When I was in high school, being nice seemed to define me. There were the jocks, the popular kids, and the bullies. I wasn't in any of those groups. I was just a regular guy. And I was nice. Being nice worked for me. (Although it was something I sometimes didn't want to hear — particularly when I asked a girl what another girl thought of me: It didn't bode well if the answer was, "She thinks you're nice," or worse, "She thinks you have a nice personality.")

As a grown-up, being nice has continued to come naturally to me in most situations. Still, as I got older I started to become irritated and annoyed by more things and I found that I wasn't as nice all the time. I wasn't happy about not being so nice, so I began actively working toward being nicer. Overall, being nice has served me well. Nice people *don't* finish last.

✳ Being Nice for a Better Life
It's easy to see how being happy, the subject of Chapter 1, is connected to having a better life. Our quest of happiness is intertwined with al-

most everything we do. Daniel Gilbert, the Harvard professor who wrote *Stumbling on Happiness* (mentioned in Chapter 1), said about studying happiness, "Why study anything else? It's the holy grail. We're studying the thing that all human action is directed toward." The benefits — to *you* — of being nice may not be as obvious, but they're equally important.

In *The Likeability Factor,* Tim Sanders (author of several very good books) reports on a study of high school students conducted by Van Sloan, a researcher and management consultant. The study was an attempt to determine how personality traits impacted popularity, and it found that the dominant factors were not, as one might have expected, attractiveness, intelligence, and athletic ability. Sloan's result showed that students had a better chance of becoming more likable by having an upbeat, positive personality; smiling; and liking other people. As you can imagine, this really hit home for me, considering what I was like in high school. And unless you want to be like Ebenezer Scrooge, you'll probably agree that being more likable is better than the alternative.

In addition to making you more likable, being nice can improve your life in many other ways. In this chapter I'll discuss how being nice will help you avoid misunderstandings, have a more pleasant home life, and reduce how frequently you get angry. And while this is not a psychology book, it's worthwhile to note that one oft-prescribed recommendation for combating depression is to help other people; if you become outwardly focused, you leave yourself less time to ruminate about your own troubles. That's useful information for all of us.

✳ Teach Your Children Well

As I explained in Chapter 1, Be Happy, my dad was my earliest teacher regarding two rules that have largely shaped my philosophy of life: He helped me learn not to sweat the small stuff when he explained to me the relative unimportance of a car, and he helped me learn how important it is to find a career you're passionate about when he told me that you have to love what you do.

As a grown-up, working with my dad, I came to learn what a nice person he is — everyone loves my dad — but as a kid, I spent much more time with my mom, and she was my earliest teacher on being nice. She was like many moms. She would do anything for us. She made breakfast, lunch and dinner every day, prepared after-school snacks for me and my friends, and wrote us a letter every single day we were away at summer camp. (And if my mom and dad went away while we were at camp, she would prewrite a bunch of letters and have a neighbor mail one each day to make sure that during their trip there was no gap in our receiving her letters.) My mom's warmhearted behavior hasn't been toward just us — she also volunteered to tutor local kids and "adopted" them into our family by having them stay for dinner; she took care of my grandfather when he developed Alzheimer's (we called it senility back then); she teaches ESL (English as a Second Language) as a volunteer; and she reads to seniors. If it's true that you inherit baldness from your mother's father, I have him to thank for my bald head, but I also have him to thank for making my mom the wonderful mom she was to her kids — and for making me and my siblings nice people. He was the nicest person I ever met, and when you teach your children, you are, in effect, teaching your grandchildren.

✳ Remember the Golden Rule

The suggestion "be nice" is not a new one. The Golden Rule, "do unto others as you would have them do unto you," has been around a long time — someone back then obviously felt that people needed to be told to be nice. Plenty has been written more recently about being nice, including books devoted entirely to the subject.

"Do unto others…" requires empathy. As Sanders explains in, *The Likeability Factor*, empathy is the ability to imagine yourself in the place of another and from that vantage point understand his feelings (whereas sympathy means your heart goes out to them, but those are *your* feelings, not their feelings).

✳ The Substitute Teacher, My First Empathy Lesson

One afternoon when I came home from elementary school and my mom asked me how school had been that day, I told her that we hadn't done much because we had a substitute teacher (a "sub"). I explained that all of us students weren't very cooperative with, or nice to, the sub, as was the norm when we had a sub. My mom said, "I bet that woman has kids at home. How do you think those kids would feel if they knew your whole class was so disrespectful to their mom?" I suddenly pictured my mom in front of my class as the sub — kids talking; kids throwing things; kids being completely disrespectful. It didn't feel good. Bam! Empathy. From that day on, I looked at subs with a different pair of eyes. I put myself in their shoes — or at least in their kids' shoes. As Linda Kaplan Thaler and Robin Koval advise in their book, *The Power of Nice*, you should treat everyone as if they are the most important person in the world, because that is what they are, to someone.

✳ Judge Others by Intent, Not Impact

One thing that has helped me be more empathetic has been a shift in my thinking about other people's actions. When your spouse buys the wrong item at the store, what was his or her intent? Did he or she *intend* to get the wrong thing? Many of us, however, leap to annoyance by judging our spouses (and others) by the impact their error had on us. For example, if he or she bought the wrong lightbulb then you can't change the burned-out bulb on your desk lamp, which means that you're delayed in having the light you need and one of you will have to make a return trip to the store to get the proper bulb. Instead, if we judge our spouse by his or her intent — he/she intended to do the right thing — then it's easy to let the mistake go, which is exactly what we should do in the first place because it's the kind of "small stuff" we shouldn't be sweating. But so often we do sweat this stuff, which in turn becomes the fodder for so many of those stupid, unimportant, trivial fights that spouses have — that annoying bickering we wouldn't do with anyone but a family member (and especially a spouse).

Here's a real dialogue from my house:

> The mom: Are you eating?
>
> The teenage daughter: (sarcastically) No.
>
> The dad: Don't respond obnoxiously to your mom.
>
> The teenage daughter: Why would she ask me that question? I'm obviously eating.
>
> The mom: You were standing, so what I meant was, "Are you eating a meal, or just taking one bite of something?"

Even when parents mean well, which is most of the time, they can be annoying to teens. It would be so nice if teens would judge their parents by intent.

I heard the comedian Lenny Marcus say that when he showed up at his mom's front door one day she asked him, "You're here?" His reply: "No, Mom, it's a hologram of me." When he tells this story as part of a routine about his mom, it's funny. But we know what his mom really meant: "What are you doing here? We weren't expecting you." Be nice, Lenny!

✳ Seeking First to Understand

It can be a humbling and often sad experience when you realize that you misread a situation and jumped to an incorrect conclusion. We've all had situations where we've failed to seek first to understand.

Dr. JP Pawliw-Fry, co-founder of the Institute for Health & Human Potential, teaches about the impact of emotions on performance, and told a story during a terrific speech he gave at a business conference I attended. (During this speech I also learned the concept of judging others by intent and not by impact.) He told of a man in line at a supermarket. The man is in a huge rush. An older woman (seemingly a grandmother) holding a baby is in front of him in line. Because he's in a rush, he's glad to see she has only one item to purchase. When it's her turn, the cashier takes the baby, holds it, and kisses it. *This is my valuable time*, he thinks angrily. He controls himself, and when it's finally his turn, he tries to start a conversation with the cashier about the baby, planning to slip in a complaint about the delay. "Beautiful baby," he says. The cashier replies, "Thank you, she's mine. I've had to take two jobs since my husband died last month, so my mom brings the baby by once each day to hold for a few minutes." The man was probably happy that he had held his tongue.

✳ The Bald Guy in the Window

For four years I was a chaperone on my son's high school band trips. One year, we went to Orlando. My roommate was Chris, a teacher I had become friendly with during a trip to Boston the previous year. In the year since the Boston trip, he had coached my daughter's soccer team.

One night during the trip, Chris was monitoring kids at the hotel swimming pool and I was stationed near our room on the fourth floor, where most of the kids were rooming, to make sure things were under control up there. Toward the end of the evening, after checking on some kids down the hall, I returned to my room and found Chris there. My cell phone, which I had left charging on the desk, was flashing. "Wow, I have three missed calls," I said.

"That was me. I was trying to call you," Chris replied. Then he explained, "I was sitting by the pool a little while ago and when I looked up at the hotel, I see this bald guy in a blue shirt going through my clothes." (Chris' suitcase was by the window, and I was wearing a blue shirt.) "So I'm thinking, 'Singer is a sick (expletive). What the (expletive) is he doing going through my clothes?' I counted the floors to be sure it was the fourth floor and I'm saying, 'What the hell is Singer doing? He's holding up my jeans. What's he doing? Smelling my underwear?' So I called you, but you didn't answer. It was the first time on the trip that you didn't answer your cell when I called, so now I'm thinking, 'He's avoiding my calls.' So I came up to the room. You weren't in here. The blinds were closed, so I wondered if maybe it was a different room. But you could have closed them while I came upstairs. Then I looked at my clothes and they were exactly as I had left them — but you could have put them back the way you found them. Finally, I opened the blinds and looked out the window and saw that we had a view of the *parking lot*, not the pool!"

After listening to his wacky story, I surprised him by saying, "That *was* me that you saw." I explained that I had brought a large bag on the trip and my son had brought a smaller one, and that we had agreed that half-way through the trip I would take some of his dirty laundry and put it in my suitcase. So that's what I was doing. My son's bag was by the window in his room, as Chris' was in our room. And the window in my son's room, across the hall from ours, overlooked the pool. I hadn't answered my cell phone because I had left it charging in the room.

I love that story because it's funny and it was built on a series of coincidences. It's also a great example of the importance of seeking first to understand. Imagine the potential damage to my friendship with Chris if he had reached me on the phone and started yelling at me, accusing me of going through his stuff. Imagine if it had gotten around to all the kids on the trip (and then to their parents back home) that I was secretly rummaging through my roommate's clothes. And think of all the people whose reputations have been ruined because of untrue accusations.

✳ The Danger of Making Assumptions

I find that with my teens I often fail to seek first to understand. One Saturday morning, for instance, I found my daughter Julie, then 15, awake much earlier than I would have expected. I asked why she was up so early. "Because Jeremy came into my room to borrow my computer and it woke me up," she explained. I then went to find Jeremy. With some anger in my voice (but fortunately not a lot), I asked, "What are you doing going into Julie's room while she's sleeping?" He said, "I didn't think she'd wake up. You've told me that you've come into my room many times while I was sleeping to make sure I remembered to set my alarm clock." It's sort of hard to argue with "I learned from you." I was glad I hadn't gone storming in to berate him for being so inconsiderate, as I assumed he had been. He *had* considered — he just hadn't executed very well.

In a famous episode of the classic TV show *The Odd Couple*, Felix admonishes Oscar against making assumptions. "When you assume, you make an ass out of you and me," Felix explains, while writing down the word as "ass-u-me." Not making assumptions is at the heart of seeking first to understand.

I recommend you check out Don Miguel Ruiz' terrific book, *The Four Agreements*. Not making assumptions is one of his four guiding principles for finding happiness. When a group of us at my office were talking about Ruiz's book one time, one of my colleagues told this story: Her son-in-law was driving in front of a bus, which kept flashing its lights and blowing its horn. Frustrated and finally infuriated by the bus driver's aggressive tactics, he moved aside at a red light, letting the bus pull up next to him. Rolling down his window, he yelled at the bus driver, "What the (expletive) is your problem?" The bus driver, taken aback, sheepishly said, "I just wanted to tell you that one of your tires is flat." Ouch. Don't make assumptions.

✳ The Dalai Lama: A Role Model for Compassion

When I think about the Dalai Lama, I picture a person who knows how to be nice. In his book *Transforming the Mind, Teachings on Generating Compassion,* he explains that he learned as a child to counter negative emotions, such as anger and hatred, by biting his fists, because that reminded him to calm down. What a great strategy. In *Ethics for the New Millennium,* he suggests other ways to calm down when you're angry: leave the room; go for a walk; count 20 breaths. All of these help bring you into the present moment and allow you to gain the awareness you need in order to act, rather than react, as we talked about in Chapter 1.

The Dalai Lama also provides great ideas for cultivating compassion and loving kindness, as well as ways to counter or avoid hatred and anger. For example, when you realize that your wish to see someone hurt cannot harm the other person, but that those hate-filled thoughts hurt you instead, you become more inclined to do what the Dalai Lama does — view those difficult people as teachers of patience. It's not a great leap from there to the realization that many people, while responsible for their actions, don't know any other way to behave because they weren't fortunate to be raised in a good environment, as you were. That is *definitely* a compassionate way to view them.

✳ How I Learned About Compassion From Poor Spellers

I used to be intolerant of poor spellers in the workplace. I found it frustrating when these smart people were terrible spellers. It just didn't make sense to me. Then, one day, I noticed that my son, a very smart kid, was not a good speller. I saw some examples of poor spelling on his homework, so I sat with him and talked about some words to try to understand what was going on. What I realized was that he just didn't see and hear the words in his mind the way I did.

There have been several movies in recent years about kids in spelling bees (my favorite is *Spellbound*, a documentary). In these movies, you can see that some kids have an extraordinary ability to "see" the spelling of words they hear. I have a natural ability to do that, though nothing close to what those kids in the spelling bees can do. I relate it to my good sense of direction. I instinctively see a map in my mind, which helps me know which way to go. Other people have a poor sense of direction. I would never think they were stupid. Yet, until my experience with my son, I was not compassionate with poor spellers.

Being a good speller, or having a good sense of direction, isn't about being smart. It's a matter of having a particular natural ability. You may take a certain ability for granted, but someone else might be operating without it. And poor spellers have other abilities that I lack. (Note to poor spellers: To compensate, make sure you have someone else proofread your work. Computerized spell-check is good, but not as good as a human editor. Having a friend or colleague edit your work is a great example of the power of teaming up with others who excel at things that you're not good at — as we discussed in Chapter 1.)

Another lesson that I'm grateful I learned when my kids were very young is that if a child does something you don't approve of, never say, "You are stupid." Your child may do a stupid thing, but he or she is not stupid. You can tell children you're disappointed that they did a stupid thing, or a bad thing, but always remember that they are not bad people. They are good. The same principle applies to praise. Praise the behavior, not the child. When they do something well, don't say "good boy," say "good job."

In *Never Good Enough, How to Use Perfection to Your Advantage Without Letting it Ruin Your Life*, Monica Ramirez Basco advises us to avoid giving our children mixed messages. We should separate praise from critique, she says, because when children hear them together, the critique cancels out the praise.

This approach also applies to interactions with adults, as I learned in an encounter with the supervisory board of our town's swim club. It was the first time that I attended one of the swim club's board meetings. When the time came for the board to hear from "the public," I listened as one person after another voiced complaints. Each started with something to the effect of, "I love the swim club, but...." I had been planning a similar approach — I wanted to express my heartfelt gratitude about what the pool had meant to me and my family, and at the same time I was there to request a change in club policy. But I realized that if I did what everyone else did, I would nullify my positive sentiments as soon as I said "but." So when my turn came, I dove right into the reason for my presence. I asked whether the board would create a smoking area and restrict smoking to that area. The president (a smoker) was vehemently opposed. I then asked whether they would consider a small, nonsmoking area — rather than banishing the smokers, creating a safe haven for nonsmokers, particularly (from my perspective) for those of us who didn't want our kids exposed to the smoking. They told me they would consider that. I then closed by thanking them for their work on the board and telling them how much I loved the swim club, that I had taught each of my kids to swim there, and that I was getting choked up talking about it. They were all smiles and gave me a rousing ovation I won't forget.

I didn't do it that way to increase the chances of getting what I wanted. I did it that way because I didn't want my gratitude to be negated by the "but." The reception I got was an important lesson in being nice. (I can't recall whether they made any changes at the swim club that year, but some years later, without my further input, they did restrict smoking to certain areas.)

✳ How I Learned That I'm From Mars

In an effort to improve the most important relationship in my life, my relationship with my wife, I have read numerous books and have sought advice in countless conversations. When I read John Gray's book *Men Are From Mars, Women Are From Venus*, which helps men and women understand the opposite sex, I felt like he had written it after being a fly on a wall in my house. Gray's book discusses some fundamental differences between men and women, and encourages us to accept and respect those differences. For example, Gray explains that men (Martians) like to achieve results, and they rarely talk about their problems unless they need expert advice. Women (Venusians), on the other hand, like to share their feelings in an effort simply to have someone listen with empathy and interest. When a woman shares her problems with a man, he immediately goes into problem-solving mode — and often feels rejected and useless when the woman doesn't take his advice. Gray explains that she wasn't looking for advice; she just wanted a friendly ear.

Like I said, this guy must have been in my house. My wife asks my opinion all the time. It can be frustrating when she doesn't act on my input. Understanding that men and women are from different planets, so to speak, helps me deal with those frustrations better, which helps me be nicer. (For example, *not* saying, "Why are you bothering to ask me if you're not going to do what I suggest?")

✳ Smile

Don't Sweat the Small Stuff, the wonderful book by Richard Carlson, is loaded with good advice to help you to be nice. Many of his suggestions are reminiscent of Dale Carnegie's 1936 classic (yes, 1936!), *How to Win Friends and Influence People*. Carnegie provides numerous recommendations, including not criticizing, giving appreciation, and being a good listener. Both Carlson and Carnegie point out that smiling is a good thing. In Chapter 1, we talked about the incredible phenomenon of feeling happy just by smiling. But the power of smiling goes further, and smiling is a vital part of being nice. As Linda Kaplan Thaler and Robin Koval explain in *The Power of Nice*, smiling infects others with happiness, and positive moods are particularly contagious. (They cite a Yale University School of Management study as evidence.) Smile at people as you walk down the street. They will smile back at you. They can't help it. We all naturally return smiles. When they smile, they will feel happy.

Even on the phone, you can hear when someone is smiling. When I make a call to certain companies I work with, when the receptionist picks up the phone, I *hear* a smile and it makes me smile.

In addition to smiling, there are other simple gestures you can make when you pass someone. When I'm taking a walk and someone walks or jogs past me, I always wave or say hi. When I'm walking and a car gives me a wide berth, I wave to thank them. Same when I'm driving and someone lets me cut in front of them.

Your encounters with people may be brief, but your behavior in those moments can make an impact. You may at some point have heard a story about a high school freshman named Kyle (you can easily find the story on the Internet). I'm not sure whether the story is true or not, but either way, it's inspiring. One variation tells of Kyle hurrying home from school carrying a ton of things in his arms, which spill onto the sidewalk. Another young man, Mark, who is passing by, helps Kyle pick up the scattered items and, because they were heading the same way, helps Kyle carry them home.

They become friends, and years later, at their high school graduation, Kyle tells Mark that the reason he was carrying all those things that day was that he had cleaned out his school locker because he had planned to go home and kill himself that day — and that Mark's kindness had made Kyle rethink his plan, and had saved his life. Like I said, I don't know whether it's a true story or not, but even just typing it now gives me chills.

✳ Be Present and Really Listen

We have two ears and one mouth so that we can listen twice as much as we speak.

— Epictetus, 2nd-century Greek philosopher

As a salesperson, I've read more books and articles on listening than on almost any other subject. Being likable is a critical attribute for a salesperson, and being a good listener is one of the most important components of being likable. In *Conceptual Selling*, Stephen E. Heiman and Robert B. Miller taught me that good salespeople don't walk into a meeting with a prospective client and start spewing a sales pitch. Instead, they learn what the prospect needs by asking good questions and then *really* listening. As Heiman and Miller explain, this means that while the other person is talking, you're not thinking of some clever thing to say next. You are focusing on what the person says so that you can learn what they need. Other books and articles refer to this as *active* listening. By giving the other person your full attention, you are being present with them. Being present is such an important practice that many books have been written specifically about it or have treated it as a central principle (the works of Richard Carlson come to mind right away). At the same time, its significance is easily forgotten as we go about our daily lives, especially in our age of multitasking.

I'm a big fan of text messaging and e-mail, but smartphones and other electronic devices are both a blessing and a curse. While they make our lives easier in many ways, they also make it more difficult to really listen and be present. I know that I've been guilty of not being present in many situations because of portable electronic communication.

As with so many new things that we incorporate into our lives, we wonder what we did before we had these devices. As a parent, I love the fact that my kids can reach me at any time, and I take for granted the ability to communicate with them from anywhere. When I was a kid, my parents would leave us the name of the restaurant or movie theater they were going to (possibly not even the phone number), or the names and phone number of the friends they were visiting. But we *never* called them.

By the time I became a dad, we were telling our kids that they could call us on our cell phones any time they needed us. We quickly realized, after receiving incessant calls from the kids, that we had to set some rules, and we taught them the difference between *wanting* to speak with us and *needing* to speak with us. When the kids switched to texting, I embraced the new technology because it seemed so much less invasive than receiving a call. Soon, the texting, too, got out of hand, and we had to ask the kids to text us only on a "need to know" basis. Friends have told me that the best etiquette is to walk out of the room to look at messages, rather than trying to discreetly look at my phone "under the table." The thing is, if you leave the room, you are, of course, no longer present with the people you're supposed to be with. And if you stay in the room and look at your phone, you're there but not truly "present," which is even worse. It's now even "official" etiquette: Smartphones and other electronic devices are not to be used at the table, we are told in *Emily Post's Table Manners for Kids*, written by the famous etiquette expert's descendants, Cindy Post Senning and Peggy Post.

✳ Practice Single-Tasking

If you're texting "under the table," you're not listening attentively. I used to think I could do many things at the same time. I was a proud multi-tasker. But I learned that if I do more than one thing at the same time, I'm not doing any of the things as well as I can. The brain isn't capable of it. Sure, I eat my breakfast while reading the newspaper most mornings, I listen to the radio while I drive, and I fold the laundry while watching a movie on TV, but the truth is that while we may think we are doing two (or more) things at once, in reality we are flitting back and forth from one to the other, briefly being present for each, but not being fully present for either.

Edward M. Hallowell, in *CrazyBusy: Overstretched, Overbooked, and About to Snap!*, explains that doing two things at the same time is like playing tennis with two balls. You might be able to keep hitting both balls back over the net, but you would be dealing with them one at a time. And you certainly wouldn't be hitting the balls as effectively as if you were playing with only one ball. Hallowell talks in his book about "e-mail voice," that distracted tone we've all heard from someone on the other end of the phone when they start reading their e-mails at the same time as they're talking with us. Multitasking is not the best way to do anything, and it's particularly poor behavior if one of the things you're supposed to be doing is listening to someone else. It's just not nice. Don't do it.

✳ Remember Names

When I read Dale Carnegie's, *How to Win Friends and Influence People*, one thing that really stuck with me was his comment that a person's name is, to that person, the sweetest and most important sound. And yet, it happens to most of us: You meet someone at a cocktail party, or anywhere else for that matter, and you instantly forget his or her name, which isn't a very nice thing to do. When it happens to me, I feel foolish, saying to myself, "I can't believe that person just told me his name and I've already forgotten it." I used to think of it as simply a bad habit. Then I realized that it's also inconsiderate — but that I could do something about it. I resolved to listen better when people tell me their names. Because forgetting names is common, a lot has been written about it. Some people recommend that you immediately repeat the person's name: "Nice to meet you, Paul." Others suggest you create a word association with their name — a rhyming scheme or something about what the person looks like: *Tall Paul.* (I know, that's an easy example, many names are trickier. In any case, I don't use that technique, but I'm putting it out there in case you want to.) The best method is to make sure that you are *really* listening — that you sincerely care to hear the person's name — because that's what it's all about. If you immediately forget, you are sending a message that you don't care. If you care (and you should if you want to be nice), make sure to listen. And if, despite your best intentions, you *do* forget a name (it will happen at some point to most of us), ask the person again. People are usually embarrassed to do this, but it's not such a terrible thing, and most of the time the other person will appreciate that you care enough to ask.

Also, make it a point to spell and pronounce people's names correctly. One trick I figured out if you're not sure how to pronounce a name is to call the person's voice mail. Listen to how *they* say their name on their outgoing message. That's the proper pronunciation. As for spelling, ask.

✳ Don't Finish People's Sentences — and Other Etiquette

It's nice to let people finish their own sentences. This is something that I've put a lot of personal effort into. I still find myself cutting people off — finishing their sentences — but I don't do it as often as I used to, and I'm trying to stop it entirely. When you cut people off mid-sentence, you might be trying to show them that you are so totally "with" them that you know what they are going to say, but it usually comes across as you trying to show how smart you are, and it's irritating to the person you're speaking with. Even if you're right about what they're going to say, it's not a good thing to do. People love to hear themselves speak — that includes you *and* the person you're talking with. When it's their turn to talk, let them have their turn. Don't interrupt. Don't cut them off. Don't finish their sentences.

It's also easy to forget to ask people about themselves once you've gotten on a roll talking about yourself. This is another area where I've tried to improve myself. In *The Essential 55*, Ron Clark explains that you have to show others that you are as interested in them as they are in you. He gives a simple suggestion to which I can totally relate: If you are asked a question in conversation, follow your reply by asking the same question back. I can get so caught up in telling my own stories that I forget to ask others to tell me theirs. I'm a bit embarrassed to admit it, but I had to teach myself that when someone in the office on Monday morning asks about my weekend, I have to remember to ask about that person's weekend after I'm finished telling my own stories.

Clark has many more suggestions for being nice. For example, if someone bumps into you, even if it was not your fault, say, "Excuse me." I figured that one out for myself as a necessity for survival in New York. Nothing in particular happened to cause me to adopt that habit. I just started doing it. I'm not meek. I don't go through life automatically taking the blame for things that other people do. I just figured, why not say "sorry" — so I always do.

Clark also discusses door-holding etiquette. I do this one to a fault. I don't know how close behind me someone has to be for it to be appropriate for me to hold the door for them, but I err on the side of politeness. I often find someone running to get to the door I'm holding because they feel bad that I'm standing there waiting for them.

Clark goes so far as to note the difference between a push door and a pull door (hold open a pull door from the outside, go through a push door first and hold it open from the inside). I've also heard that for a revolving door, the proper etiquette is to go first, because it's a push door — your pushing makes it easier for the person behind you.

Elevators create a lot of confusion. Someone yells to you to hold the elevator. Even if you try to do it for them, you might not be able to find the "Door Open" button fast enough. But you need to try. Yes, if you hold the elevator in the lobby and the person getting on is going to a lower floor than you, then not only did you delay the elevator, but you also have an extra stop. Plus, by holding it for one person, you might end up having additional people make it onto the elevator — more waiting and more stops. But if you want to do the right thing, it's simple. Use the golden rule. What would you want them to "do unto you"? You would want them to hold the elevator for you. Do the same unto them. Hold it.

✳ Focus on Gratitude

In Chapter 1 I discussed how gratitude is an important part of being happy. Of course, expressing gratitude is also a key component of being nice. It's one of the first things we learn as a child. Someone gives us something and our mom says, "Say thank you to the nice man." It's so basic, and yet it can never be overstated: Saying thank you is critical. When you express gratitude to others, it makes them feel good. They love it. People want to be appreciated.

One of the best experiences I've had on the receiving end of gratitude was with the former president of the house of worship where my family goes. I was on the board when Helene was president, and it felt wonderful every time she thanked me for something I did — and she thanked me for everything. Every single thing that I did. Even the smallest things. And it made me want to do anything I could to help her.

Another way to express your appreciation for someone is to give a speech about them. I call it "eulogizing the living." I find funerals to be sad. I always cry. But I also find them to be inspirational. I love hearing amazing things about regular people like me — people who were not rock stars or heads of state. I hear these speeches and realize these were *not* ordinary people — they were *extraordinary* people. I find myself wanting to accomplish some of the things they did. And, if I didn't know them well, I find myself wishing I had known them better.

In *The Random House College Dictionary*, eulogy is defined as "a speech or writing in praise of a person or thing, esp. a set oration in honor of a deceased person." I always thought of eulogies as being exclusively for the deceased, but the definition shows that it can be for someone living. I say, let's not wait until someone passes away to talk about what we think about them, their wonderful personality traits, their accomplishments, and the ways that they inspire us. Tell them now, while they can appreciate it. Even better, tell it publicly. I love giving speeches at weddings, milestone birthdays, retirement lunches, and any other occasions for celebrating one of my friends or relatives. I highly recommend it.

✳ Be Intolerant of Intolerance

The popular musician, Beck, who's known for creating music that integrates rock, hip-hop, blues, and other styles, said in a *New York Times Magazine* interview, "Any kind of intolerance, I have a distaste for." I agree — I'm intolerant of intolerance. Intolerance is the cause of major world problems — nationalistic and religious intolerance, for example, are at the root of the ongoing troubles in the Middle East. (And, as you will recall from this book's introduction, one of my lifetime goals is world peace.)

Intolerance and prejudice often come from a lack of exposure to people who appear to be different from us. For example, when I was a kid, I wasn't comfortable with kids who had learning disabilities. Now I have a niece with learning disabilities and I'm not only tolerant of people like her, but also sympathetic to their needs and empathetic toward their families.

And through my exposure to my niece I gained important insight about labeling people. Her school is for children with autism and I've learned that it's not right to say that a person is autistic — it's labeling. Instead, the right thing to say is, "She has autism" or "She's a person with autism." It's a subtle difference, but an important one. By referring to someone as a person with autism, you're first calling them a person — a person like you and me — and the other part, the autism, is simply a condition or a feature, like having dark hair or light hair or no hair.

Similarly, the color of someone's skin needs to be viewed as simply a feature, like hair color. If you're in a big room, and you want to point someone out, you might say, "That guy over there, the one with the brown hair," or, "That guy over there, the one with the white shirt." Likewise, instead of saying, "That guy over there — the white guy," I would love it if we could say, "That guy over there — the one with the white skin." If you refer to him as "the white guy" or "the black guy," it's a label. If you refer to his having white skin or brown skin, it's just a feature like brown or blond hair. I know that's not how people speak, but I'd like it to be.

Sadly, there's lots of intolerance in our world regarding skin color — how insane! If I have white skin and go to Florida and sit in the sun, I'll come back with brown skin. How can people be judged by skin color?

It's hard to believe that in the United States — the country founded on life, liberty, and the pursuit of happiness; the country with a pledge of allegiance that ends "and liberty and justice for all"; the country with the Statue of Liberty as one of its major symbols; the country where, as Martin Luther King, Jr. reminded us in his "I Have a Dream" speech, our founding document includes the phrase, "We hold these truths to be self-evident, that all men are created equal" — it's hard to believe that just a few decades ago people who didn't have white skin had to sit in the back of buses, had to drink from separate water fountains, and weren't served in most restaurants. That's sick.

King famously said, in that same speech, "I have a dream that my four little children will one day live in a nation where they will not be judged by the color of their skin but by the content of their character." Unfortunately, as we know, there's still too much judging by the color of one's skin and by other things that are equally unimportant — as unimportant as the color of one's hair.

In *Man's Search for Meaning*, Viktor Frankl, the concentration camp survivor, similarly talked of judging people on their character when he said that the world is divided into two races — the "race" of the decent man and the "race" of the indecent man. Some of the indecent men he referred to were those who tortured and killed concentration camp prisoners due to their religion, nationality, or sexual orientation.

When the Dalai Lama won the 1989 Nobel Peace Prize, he began his lecture at the award ceremony by saying that as he travels all around the world, he is constantly reminded that we are all basically alike and that wearing different clothes, having different skin color, or speaking different languages are just surface things. "But basically, we are the same human beings."

Joe Louis is considered by many to have been the finest heavyweight champion in the history of boxing. He held the world's heavyweight title from 1937 until 1948 and successfully defended his title a record 25 times. More important, he was a great man, making numerous contributions to society. He also had brown skin. The sportswriter Jimmy Cannon said, "Louis is a credit to his race — the human race." I love that quote. That says it all.

✳ New Habits and Progress

Remember: *Life is long*, meaning we have time. If we try to make a million changes all at once, we often end up so overwhelmed that we make none. Instead, if we *slow down to make the changes*, and then *stop to celebrate the progress*, we'll accomplish much more.

Slow Down to Make the Changes — It takes 21 days to form a new habit. What are some ideas you have for new habits you would like to adopt following your reading of Chapter 2?

Stop to Celebrate the Progress — Remember to look back on all that you've accomplished. What are some areas of progress you've made?

Chapter 3
Be a Leader

A woman and her son travel across India to see Gandhi. After waiting hours to speak with him, she asks Gandhi to tell her son to stop eating sugar. Gandhi asks her to come back in a week. A week later, she again travels to see Gandhi. Again, she asks Gandhi to tell her son to stop eating sugar. Gandhi tells the child, "Son, stop eating sugar." The mother asks Gandhi why they had to wait a week and travel so far two times. Gandhi replies, "A week ago, I was still eating sugar."

Max De Pree, former CEO of furniture maker Herman Miller and author of *Leadership is an Art*, says that while people may listen to preaching, it's behavior that they emulate. Gandhi was a great leader for many reasons, including the fact that he led by example — he practiced what he preached. "We must become the change we wish to see," he famously said.

When I told a close friend about the *Six Simple Rules*, he said, "I don't think everyone can be a leader." It's true that when we think of leaders we often think of presidents, CEOs, and heroic figures such as Martin Luther King, Jr. and Gandhi. But leadership is also making the world a better place, even in "small" ways, and we all have it in us to do that. We can all be leaders — leaders in our community; leaders of others; leaders of ourselves. Being a leader can mean so many things. It's about the role you play in your family. It's about getting involved in your community and coaching your kids' sports teams. It's about setting an example and taking on responsibility.

Much of what we've discussed so far in this book is about leadership. By choosing to be happy and changing your thinking, you're taking a leadership role in your happiness. And I chose *Be a Leader* as my third rule, directly after *Be Nice*, because to me they are close cousins. My definition of leadership includes many activities that enhance the lives of others and, as we discussed in the previous chapter, helping others is one way to be nice and is one of the keys to happiness and a better life. In Chapter 6, we'll talk about taking a leadership role in your health. This chapter is about being a leader in all ways.

✳ Bigger Than Yourself

As discussed in Chapter 1, working for a cause bigger than yourself is one of the secrets to being happy. It's also one of the most significant ways that you can be a leader. People who are dedicated to a larger cause are the leaders we need to make the world a better place. Gandhi spent his life working for something bigger than himself. He wasn't fighting for his own freedom. He was fighting to achieve independence for India and to help the poor.

I enjoy reading biographies of people who have committed themselves to these types of goals — U.S. presidents, for example. Presidents may enjoy the power, but the things they accomplish are not for themselves. They help change the world (hopefully for the better) in ways that go far beyond themselves.

Richard Nixon, though he resigned the presidency in disgrace, was a respected statesman in his later years. At the 1990 dedication of his presidential library he said, "Only when you become engaged in a cause greater than yourself, can you be true to yourself." The struggle for civil rights in the United States is even more inspirational than presidential biographies. Martin Luther King, Jr. sacrificed way too much to have been doing it for himself. His goals were much larger than that. "An individual has not started living," King said, "until he can rise above the narrow confines of his individualistic concerns to the broader concerns of all humanity."

The civil rights movement was driven by people who rose to fight for the greater good. In *The Children*, David Halberstam wrote about the sit-ins in Nashville, and the young college students who were propelled into the movement's leadership. Each one, Halberstam writes, was inspired and empowered by fighting for a cause bigger than himself or herself. In a defining moment of a debate among civil rights leaders in 1961, one of those students, John Lewis (who went on to a career in public service and has been a congressman since 1987) paraphrased the Jewish sage Hillel when he asked: "If not us, then who? If not now, then when? Will there be a better day for it tomorrow or next year? Will it be less dangerous then? Will someone else's children have to risk their lives instead of us risking ours?"

✹ It's About Helping Other People

Booker T. Washington, who fought his way out of slavery to become an educator and political leader, wrote in his 1900 autobiography, *Up From Slavery,* that "those who are happiest are those who do the most for others."

Mother Teresa is the poster person for helping others. Everybody should read a Mother Teresa biography to be inspired. There are so many wonderful, instructive stories about her. In one story, Mother Teresa was attending to a cancer patient who reeked so badly that he asked her how she was able to stand the smell. "It's nothing," she is said to have replied, "compared to the pain you must feel."

In 2009, the New York Mets named its new baseball stadium's entry pavilion the Jackie Robinson Rotunda after the brave player who broke Major League Baseball's color barrier when he joined the Brooklyn Dodgers in 1947. The Mets chose this Robinson quote to grace the wall of the pavilion: "A life is not important except in the impact it has on other lives."

When my friend Mark nominated me for *NJBIZ* magazine's "Forty Under 40" program, he wrote, "David has a competitive drive to improve the lives of everyone he touches." That is one of my proudest moments. While I can't put myself in the class with the heroes I've talked about above, I very much aspire to be like them.

✳ It's Easier to Raise a Million Dollars Than a Thousand

My niece Rebecca, daughter of my brother Jon, was born with a rare genetic disorder and she has special needs. Jon will do almost anything to make sure her needs are met. However, rather than focus exclusively on Rebecca, Jon decided to help the larger community of children with special needs and their families. He formed an organization, called *The Drive for Rebecca,* to increase awareness of autism, raise desperately needed funds for autism research and education, and create a school where Rebecca and other children could learn and grow to the best of their abilities. He and others raised nearly $100,000, provided funds to support medical research, and donated money to leading educational programs for children with autism. Jon ultimately joined forces with five other local families to start REED Academy, in Garfield, New Jersey, and

Drive for Rebecca donated funds to help establish another school. REED opened in 2003, and because of the miracles that happen there every day, five students have graduated and are attending their local elementary schools together with their typically developing peers. Jon once told me that it's easier to raise $1,000,000 than to raise $1,000. What he meant was that when you are raising money for a personal cause, it has limited appeal. But when your cause is larger than yourself, you've got a much better story to tell.

✳ There are So Many Ways to Help Others

My friend Colleen O'Donnell (along with her friend Lyn Baker) wrote a wonderful book called *Generous Kids* about "helping your child experience the joy of giving." Their book provides ideas and resources for helping children ages 3-18 become "generous kids" — which can have far-reaching effects. In its 2002 report *Engaging Youth in Lifelong Service*, Independent Sector, an organization devoted to advancing the philanthropic community, found that people who begin giving and volunteering as youths are much more likely to donate time and money as adults, and that those who have a role model who volunteers become the most generous adults. This highlights the powerful impact that you can have on the world by encouraging your children to be "generous kids," and, even more so, by leading by example — being generous with your time, talent, and money.

I've never thought of myself as someone who has given a ton to my community, yet when I add it all up it's been quite a lot: coaching my kids' sports teams; chaperoning my kids' school trips; serving as a board member and officer of my religious institution; writing reviews of parenting books for the PTA newsletter; speaking at schools to share some of the advice that turned into this book; attending board of education meetings; preparing meals at a homeless shelter; sleeping at the homeless shelter (they need two volunteers every night); donating groceries to food drives; pledging money to friends and family members who have participated in 5K races, marathons, triathlons, bike rides, and the like; and quite a bit more. There are so many ways to help others.

✳ Start Small

Stories about leaders are inspiring, but they can also be intimidating. "How can I possibly be as great as Mother Teresa?" you may ask yourself. But no one is asking you to be the next Mother Teresa. Start small. As Napoleon Hill, author of the classic *Think and Grow Rich,* said, "If you cannot do great things, do small things in a great way." The ever-modest Mother Teresa herself said, "We cannot do great things on this Earth, only small things with great love." Most people think of philanthropy as giving money. But the roots of the word are the Greek "philos," which means loving, and "anthropos," meaning man. Philanthropy is loving others by helping them in any way. Dictionary.com defines the word as "an altruistic concern for human welfare and advancement, usually manifested by donations of money, property, or work to needy persons, by endowment of institutions of learning and hospitals, and by generosity to other socially useful purposes." I once read that a hero is a person who is interested in making the world a better place. Love others. Help others. Be a philanthropist. Be a hero.

✳ Getting Involved

You can be a leader and get involved in your community in many ways. Sometimes it's a matter of standing up for what you think is right. For example, I'm proud of my effort to get my local school district to observe Martin Luther King, Jr. Day, which was first observed in 1986. But it took several years for companies to adopt it as a day off. In the mid-'90s we decided at my company to close our office on MLK Day. My kids were very young the first time we did it and because they had school that day, I went to pick them up. That night, I wrote a letter to the board of education urging them to close our schools on MLK Day the following year, explaining that the day was becoming accepted as a standard national holiday — judging by, among other things, the number of dads who picked up their kids at school that day (moms were the norm on other days). The board wrote back to me asking me to present my recommendation at its next meeting. I did so, and board members discussed their feelings on the subject. They pointed out that the school had been closed a couple of years earlier on MLK Day, but that it had been a snowy winter that year, with many unexpected days off for snow, so the board had reversed course and decided it could not continue giving MLK Day off while still meeting New Jersey's strict requirement for the number of days of school each year. I explained my concern was that we were not setting a good example for our kids by having school on MLK Day, rather than demonstrating the respect that Dr. King deserved. The board voted to make MLK Day a school holiday for the following year, as well as for all future years (meaning they would not change their mind if there were too many snow days again).

When my kids went to high school, we were part of a larger, regional district, which had its own calendar and its own board of education. I was surprised to find that our high school district did not observe MLK Day, so I wrote to the high school's board of education. The superintendent wrote back, explaining that instead of having a day off, the school had a day of learning about Dr. King. After MLK Day of my son's freshman year, I asked him about the program. He reported that the day had very little MLK-related learning. I wrote again to the superintendent, who explained that two of my son's teachers had been out that day and that the substitutes did not have the proper curriculum. I wasn't happy with the answer, but accepted the promise that the next year would be different. A year later, it wasn't any different. So I wrote again. Finally, for my son's junior year — and beyond — the board voted for a half day off, with the morning dedicated to classes about Dr. King. I was not entirely satisfied, but it was progress, and I had accomplished part of my goal — the half day would make it clear to the kids that Dr. King deserved special recognition.

✳ Your Obituary

One method I like for thinking about lifetime goals, a method that I've read about in many places, is to write your obituary now. What do you want it to say? What contributions will you have made to the world? How will you have made a difference? One thing you never read in someone's obituary is, "He worked a lot." What you read is what a wonderful husband or wife, father or mother, grandfather or grandmother, son or daughter, friend, and/or sibling this person was — and what contributions he or she made to the community, society, and the world.

There's a great poem called "The Dash," by Linda Ellis, which beautifully expresses this idea. The "dash" is the dash between the years on your tombstone — between the year of your birth and the year of your passing. The poem challenges you to think about that dash — about how you want to spend your time here and what kind of impact you want to make on the world. Read the poem. It's inspiring. (You can Google it or you can go to www.lindaellis.net/Read_The_Dash.htm.)

We don't know what that second year on our tombstone is going to be. If you want to accomplish something, do it now. Another poem that you should read, called "If I Knew," by George Michael Grossman, talks about the things you might do if you knew you were seeing someone you love for the last time. None of us is promised a tomorrow, the poem tells us, so rather than waiting until tomorrow to do those things, we should do them today.

Leaders don't put off to tomorrow what they can do today, especially the important things. As I wrote in this book's introduction, I agree with the saying "Life is short" because the years fly by and each part of your life is short relative to the entirety of your life — for example, the child-rearing years, which are such a major phase, are really a small percent of your life, just as your own childhood, when you look back, was a small amount of time. So you have to make the most of each moment. But life is also long in the sense that you can spend more time at work later, when your kids have moved out. Do the *meaningful* things now.

✳ My Advice to New Dads

One important reason why being a parent is so meaningful is that it's bigger than yourself. You are focusing entirely on someone else. Here is some advice I've given to many dads-to-be whose wives were going to stay at home taking care of the children, at least for a while. (This advice is for mom if it's dad who will be staying at home.)

If your child does not sleep through the night, and most don't for quite a few months, you are going to be running on a less-than-ideal amount of sleep. Here's how to deal with it: Remember that this is a relatively short period of time in a long life and you'll eventually catch up on your sleep. If your wife wants you to get up in the middle of the night to help with the baby, *do it*. You might be tempted to say something like, "I have to wake up in the morning and go to work to earn the money that allows you to stay at home all day." Don't say that. Don't think that. (And *definitely* don't say anything suggesting that your wife is "at home all day doing nothing.")

Here's how I learned this lesson. About eight months after our twin daughters were born, things became really rough in the middle of the nights at our house. We had a 3-year-old son, and our 8-month-old daughters were waking up many times each night. Up until that time, when Marcie would ask me to handle any nighttime feedings, I almost always said something like, "I have to get up for work and you can sleep during the day." Because she was never much of a napper, and in any case had a lot to do when the kids were napping during the day, I was totally wrong when I said, "You can sleep during the day." I understood how difficult the nights were because occasionally I did help out and it could be incredibly frustrating. But I did not truly appreciate how much Marcie was doing, and what it was like for her. This is a brief conversation we had one morning:

David: Wow! The kids finally slept through the night last night!

Marcie: No; *you* slept through the night.

One day, when it had gotten really bad for Marcie, I decided that I would handle the nighttime feedings. I'm not sure what prompted it, but I kind of said to myself, "Be a leader, get up, stop whining about needing sleep, just do it." And I did it.

It wasn't easy. But soon I actually started enjoying it. I was working long hours in the office, often leaving the house before the kids woke up in the morning, so I began to treasure holding them in the middle of the night. I knew I had become the official nighttime person when one morning Marcie and I had this exchange:

Marcie: The kids finally slept through the night last night!

David: No; *you* slept through the night.

It continued this way for years. By giving Marcie the gift of sleep, I gave myself a whole set of beautiful memories, and a special bond with my kids that will always be there. When the girls became old enough to climb out of their beds and come to our room in the middle of the night, they came to my side of the bed — even though it was farthest from the door — because I had become the go-to nighttime parent. I'll always remember that. The lost sleep I recovered from and forgot about soon enough.

✳ Jim Kelly's Lessons

I began helping with my kids' sports teams as soon as my oldest was in kindergarten. I decided pretty quickly (after the very first "kindergarten clinic" soccer session) that I didn't want to be the head coach. The reason was that my son wouldn't listen to me. The other kids did, but mine didn't. There was enough of that at home, and I didn't want to add more of it if I didn't have to. Instead, every year when the forms came to sign up my kids, in the place where you could note your interest in coaching I wrote "assistant coach." (I'm not sure if I inspired the change, but a number of years later a line appeared on the form where parents could specifically request an assistant coaching position.)

I was an assistant coach for soccer, basketball, and baseball for my son, and soccer, basketball, and softball for my daughters. When my daughters were in fourth grade, I received a call:

> "David, I wanted to let you know that you're going to be your daughters' basketball head coach this season — the third- and fourth-grade team."
>
> "No, you don't understand," I countered. "I'm the assistant coach."
>
> "No, *you* don't understand. We don't have anyone else to do it. You're the head coach."

After a 10-minute conversation/pep talk, I relented. In addition to my concern about my kids not listening to me, I was worried about my lack of experience because I had never played much basketball. I was comforted, however, by the fact that the head coach of the prior year's team, Jim Kelly, had done an awesome job, and I had learned a lot while helping him. (Jim's daughter was now in fifth grade, and Jim was going to be coaching her fifth-and sixth-grade team.) I had written up notes about some of the things he did (see Chapter 4, Be Organized — write everything down!) in anticipation of assisting a different head coach when my girls were in fourth grade. I had prepared to be the best assistant coach ever. Instead, I was going to be the head coach. So I called Jim and asked him for advice, and he gave me quite a few helpful tips.

The season went well. We won six games and lost five. The 10 girls on my team had fun and made a lot of progress. I had fun and learned a lot.

The following season, when my daughters were to be fifth graders, I planned to be an assistant coach again, for the fifth- and sixth-grade team. I hoped to work again with Jim, and then perhaps I would return to head coaching the following year.

Once again, though, my tidy plans were derailed. Someone asked me whether there was going to be a fifth-grade "travel" team that year. A travel team is a higher-level team that travels to other towns for games. I started asking around and the answer I got was, "To have a team, the first step is someone needs to be the coach." So I tried to recruit several other parents for the coaching position. None agreed, and after a few weeks I decided to do it.

The experience provided many lessons in leadership. We won only one game and lost 11. Ouch. But, despite the terrible record, the girls had fun. The losing wasn't fun, but a nice camaraderie developed, and they made a lot of progress, individually and as a team. We lost the first game, 30-6, the second game, 19-13, which actually gave us some confidence, and then we lost the next few games by similar scores. I called Jim to see whether he had any thoughts on what I could do. He gave me a great idea, which led to some important, small victories.

One game, when we were clearly out of it after three quarters (down 24-4), I had this conversation with the girls:

"Do you think we have a chance to win this game?"

One or two said yes (probably because they thought it was the right thing to say), and the rest said no. "You're right," I said. "We have almost no chance of winning this game." (Though I didn't say it to them, our team was, as usual, much shorter and less experienced than the opposition, and we had a less experienced coach — me. We had asked to be in the lowest skill level, but we were placed in the second of three divisions, where we were overmatched all year. If we were losing by a lot in a game, our chances of coming back and winning were slim.)

"Let's say this game is over," I told them. "Now let's start a new game. It's going to last one quarter. Let's see if we can beat this team for one quarter."

And we won the fourth quarter, 12-0. It was remarkable. We scored more in that quarter than we had in any prior quarter — or in all four quarters combined in many of our previous games. I was so inexperienced and oblivious that I didn't even realize that the other team had its second-stringers in, but that didn't matter anyway. That quarter was a great victory for the girls.

Although we kept losing, we were able to achieve several similar "victories." When the season was near its end, we got creamed by the team that eventually went on to win the league championship. They were winning 21-4 at the half, and went on to win 25-10. This time, I didn't point out to the girls our small victory — we had won the second half 6-4. But they pointed it out to me! What a feeling. Ten-year-olds having this perspective — what an achievement!

We did win one game before losing our last two of the season, but in one of the final games the score was 31-24 — the 24 points were the most we had scored by far, which was another small victory the girls recognized. I asked them, "If we could go back in time and play against our beginning-of-the-season selves, who would win?" They quickly announced that it was obvious — they were much better now.

Those small victories made it clear to me that (to use a variation of a famous phrase) it's not whether you win or lose, but *that* you play the game. It was important that the girls got out there and played because they wanted to play, they wanted to improve, and they wanted to have fun — and they got to do all three. This was one of the many leadership lessons I came away with from this experience. To be a good leader, you need to instill confidence in the people you're leading. You need to give them something to fight for, to play for, and you need to find small successes to build on. I'm very competitive and want to win as much as anyone. But there are ways to measure success and progress beyond whether you win or lose. If you can feel successful without "winning," you will most certainly have a better life, and if you help others around you — in this case, the kids you are coaching — to feel successful, you will improve their lives as well. Perception is reality — if you feel successful, you *are* successful. Those kids were successful, and that was fulfilling for me.

✳ Keep Score as a Family

When my son was 5 years old I had learned a similar lesson about being a leader within my family. A friend suggested that when my family played sports together we should add up the total of everyone's scores, rather than tracking individual scores.

I used that method to make sure all the sports we played were fun. With tennis, instead of playing against each other we counted how many times we could hit the ball back and forth without hitting it out or into the net. We did the same with badminton, Ping-Pong, and a beach paddle game called Kadima. When we bowled, we totaled our scores and compared the total against prior outings, each time trying to beat our best family score. When we played basketball in our driveway, we tried to see how many shots we could get in as a group.

✳ Youth Sports Gone Bad

In July of 2000, in suburban Boston, Michael Costin was supervising his three sons and several other boys in a pickup hockey game. Thomas Junta's son was one of the boys in the game and after Junta objected to rough play during the game, the two men fought. At the end of the fight, Michael Costin, 40, was dead. A year and a half later, in January of 2002, Thomas Junta, 44, was sentenced to six-to-10 years in jail for the beating death of Michael Costin.

Parents' behavior at youth sports events provides a great example of the importance of good leadership. When my daughter was 11, I witnessed one incident of aggressive behavior by parents and was involved in another, although thankfully neither one ended as dramatically or tragically as the Costin-Junta affair. Nothing happened that would merit mention in the newspaper. But things could have gotten much uglier, and these incidents included poor behavior by me and others and demonstrated the lack of leadership found too often these days in the area of youth sports.

In the first incident, a parent of one of my daughter's soccer teammates nearly came to blows with one of the opposing team member's parents. Levelheaded parents were able to get in between them before anything violent happened. I was relatively far from the incident, sitting atop the bleachers, and called the police when the trouble started. When the police arrived (after things had already calmed down), one of the officers spoke with the other team's parents, telling them, "If I have to come down here again, I'll arrest you." I was thinking that he should have spoken with our team's parents as well, but I guess you just need to talk to one side, because it takes two to tango — which is a good leadership lesson — it only takes one to be the leader, to do the right thing to avoid problems.

Before the next game, the coach of my daughter's team met with parents to tell us that we had to take a leadership role by controlling ourselves and staying calm. He was so right. Emotions run high when it comes to our children and tempers can flare; but all the while, our kids are watching and learning. It's up to us to teach them the right way to behave.

Yet, only two weeks later, I failed. My daughter's team was involved in a particularly physical soccer game, with lots of pushing and two yellow cards (warnings) for the other team. The other team's parents were sniping at the ref. Then my daughter was knocked to the ground by an elbow to the face, and she had to be helped off the field. Instead of keeping my cool and setting a good example, I blew up, yelling and cursing. All my behavior did was escalate a tense situation into one that could have become violent. It was critical that I learn from the incident and not let it happen again. I had to be a leader and set a good example for the other parents and for the kids. And I'm happy to say that nothing like that happened with me, or anyone else, at any game I was at over subsequent years.

✳ Don't Use Profanity

In addition to everything else I did wrong in the previous story, I used profanity — definitely a problem of mine. The legendary Bill Veeck, who owned several Major League Baseball teams during his lifetime, wrote in his autobiography, *Veeck — As In Wreck*, that he learned from his father not to use foul language. His dad had told him that people use "cusswords" when they can't think of anything else to say and that using them shows people that you're stupid. Veeck said that though he was not a prude and he didn't care how his friends spoke, it became a matter of personal pride for him to find the right words to express what he wanted to say. Sage advice we should all learn from and emulate. As the saying goes, "Strong and bitter words indicate a weak cause."

✳ Life is Short *and* Life is Long

Now that I've told you how not to behave at your kids' games, I want to urge you to go to as many games as you can. This is the type of thing people have in mind when they say that we should go out and do things because "life is short." But the way to make progress in this area is to realize that life is actually long.

It's important to realize that you'll have a very long time after the relatively few years when your children are young. Let's do the math. Say you have three kids, with the oldest and youngest five years apart. Your oldest starts having lots of activities for you to attend when she is 4. Five years later, your youngest starts with her activities, which continue for around 13 years, give or take a couple of years. That makes a total of 18 years. Meanwhile, a typical career lasts more than 40 years.

If you put your kids' games, school events, and other activities on your calendar — if you choose to make them a priority — you'll never regret it. Many people regret missing their kids' activities. Don't be one of those people. If our work is full of activities we are great at and love to do (see Chapter 1), we won't be in a rush to retire, so we'll have plenty of time to catch up on the work after we sacrifice it somewhat during the years we are focusing on our kids.

When you go to many games and events, there's always room to miss one if you really have to. You'll feel bad, but you won't feel guilty. It's the parents who repeatedly find themselves apologizing to their kids for missing an event who feel guilty. If your kids see you at most of their performances and games, it will mean the world to them, and they'll understand when you have to miss one.

✳ Honesty

There are many good aphorisms about honesty. There is no doubt that "honesty is the best policy." I also like the saying, "When you tell the truth, you only have to remember one story." That's aptly illustrated by a story about four college friends who go away for a ski weekend right before finals. They party heavily, which causes them to return to school too late to take their first exam. They find their professor and explain that they had gone away for a weekend of skiing and studying and, unfortunately, had a flat tire on the way back, didn't have a spare, and were stranded so long that they missed the final. The professor thinks for a moment and readily agrees that they can make up the final the following day. The friends are happy and relieved. They study that night and show up the next day at the appointed time. They are placed in separate rooms and handed a test booklet. The first question, worth five points, is simple. Each student zips through it and then turns the page to read the next question: "For 95 points: Which tire?"

I remember my first brush with dishonesty. Around age 5, I came home from a walk with my grandfather. My mom saw me take a piece of gum out of my pocket, and asked me whether my grandfather had bought it for me. I told her the truth — that I had just taken it from a store. My mom explained to me about stealing and made me go back to the store with my grandfather to give it back. Despite my limited understanding of the situation, I remember being extremely nervous and embarrassed, and then appreciative that my grandfather let me put the gum back without telling the store owner that I had taken it in the first place. It's good to get that kind of thing out of the way at a young age.

As an adult, what I continue to struggle with in the honesty arena is white lies. When my son, Jeremy, was a freshman in high school, he decided to try out for the tennis team. He felt he was a long shot but decided to try out nonetheless. It rained the morning of the second day of tryouts. He assumed the tryout was canceled, so he walked home after school. Later, when Marcie got home, she asked Jeremy why he wasn't at tennis tryouts. After he explained, she told him that she had driven by the high school earlier and had seen the team playing. When I got home that night and heard the story, I asked him what he was going to tell the coach the next day. He said he was going to tell the truth — and I realized that my son always told the truth, and I was grateful. My instinctive reaction was thinking that he should come up with a story to cover for his mistake, but I was glad I didn't say that. I knew that my kids were going to find themselves in many similar situations in the years to come and I vowed to myself that I would encourage them to always tell the truth.

My friend Michele has been an inspiration for me regarding cutting out white lies, and I once asked her how she does it. I used the example of being at someone's house, not enjoying the food, and being asked how you like what was served — a situation in which I had certainly told white lies. Michele uses a brilliant strategy: She compliments something she *does* like before the host has a chance to ask. For example, she might not like the main dish, so she will say, "These roasted vegetables are delicious."

Cutting out white lies is a common challenge. I read a column in 2009 that lamented the in-your-face truthfulness in the world of blogging and the like, and encouraged "little white lies" rather than making someone feel bad. It even used the dinner-at-someone's-house example and repeated the traditional "Be Nice" advice: "If you don't have anything nice to say, don't say anything at all."

It seems to me that sometimes, if you don't have anything nice to say, you need to tell a white lie. But drawing the line between total honesty and "necessary" white lies is tricky. I had an e-mail conversation with my sister-in-law, Michey, about white lies, and one of her comments exemplified how conflicted many of us are about them. Michey said: "I don't tell white lies...Unless it is to Sam [her then 9-year-old son]... Well, maybe to avoid hurting someone's feelings — maybe about their clothes or something."

✳ Don't Say "To Be Honest With You"

Another good piece of honesty advice is to avoid using the phrases: "to be honest with you"; "honestly"; "to tell you the truth"; "I'm going to be straight with you"; "I'm not going to lie to you"; and other similar qualifiers. Many years ago, someone told me that if you say those things, the person you're talking to will wonder why you have to tell them you're being honest — is it because you're usually *not* honest with them and you need to alert them that this time you're telling the truth? Many people accept those phrases as figures of speech, used to emphasize a point, not as reflections on a person's honesty. Nonetheless, I highly recommend that you stop using those expressions. I did, and now I cringe when I hear someone else using them. When someone says, "to be perfectly honest with you," I think to myself, sarcastically, "Are you sure you wouldn't rather lie?"

✳ Keeping Secrets

When a person confides in you, you can't tell anyone what they shared with you. How many times has someone told you something that they were supposed to keep as a secret, and then they ask *you* to keep it as a secret? A friend (we'll call him Fred) might say to me: "David, listen, I'm going to tell you something, but you can't tell anyone. Kim and

Max might be getting a divorce. Max told me in confidence, so you can't tell anyone."

That drives me nuts. If Max told Fred not to tell anyone, why is Fred telling me? Because he thinks he can trust me. From here, it's easy to imagine a chain of events where I go on to tell someone else the secret, asking them to be sure not to tell anyone else, and then that person tells someone else, and before long, everyone knows the "secret." The originator of the story, in this case Max, confided in Fred perhaps because he wanted to share it with someone — to get advice, to get it off his chest, just to have someone to talk to about his troubling situation. Fred has to keep the information to himself. When someone tells me something in confidence, I don't tell anyone. Not even my wife. (I know that people often feel that sharing something with a spouse doesn't count as breaking a promise of secrecy — that an important part of a relationship with a spouse is being able to tell him or her anything. But I find it easier to strictly follow the "don't tell anyone" rule than to make any exceptions — and my wife does the same.)

If you share someone's secret, you're obviously violating that person's trust. But the damage goes beyond that. If you keep telling people things that you're supposed to keep secret, then *those* people will stop trusting you because they'll know that you're likely to break their confidence.

At the house of worship where I'm a member, we had a big blowup around the issue of keeping information private. At our board meetings, an attorney who ran the legal committee would give a short speech about the importance of maintaining strict confidentiality regarding any personnel discussions. One time, after such a speech, the president announced some actions that had been taken by the officers. Some board members protested having been kept in the dark about these actions. The president explained that due to past leaks, the officers felt it necessary to deliberate and carry out these particularly sensitive personnel actions without consulting the full board. Several board members persisted about how unhappy they were to have been left out of the loop. I jumped in and said I felt strongly that if the officers (I was not an officer) could not trust us to keep discussions secret, they had no choice but to exclude us. I said I was disgusted and outraged that people in that room were leaking information and explained that I didn't even tell my wife what went on at the meetings.

For quite a while after that meeting, we didn't have any problems with leaks. I wish I could say that the problem was gone for good, but it arose again a number of years later when the board confronted a controversial issue. Again, I was sickened by it, and the leaks did irreparable damage to the board's ability do quality work, as some board members announced they would never again be comfortable expressing their opinions "in confidence" on potentially controversial topics.

Leaders keep secrets they are supposed to keep, which made these incidents particularly galling for me because this group was the lay *leadership* of the institution. I'm sure my experience is not uncommon, which is a shame. When you volunteer to serve on a board, you are being a leader and helping both the organization and the people it serves. But you have to take your job seriously, and keeping confidential information private is part of that job — just as it is a part of your "job" of being a friend.

✳ Don't Gossip

Who gossips to you will gossip of you. — Turkish proverb

In the preceding section I wrote that if you tell people things that you're supposed to keep secret, then those people will stop trusting you because they'll know you're the type who doesn't keep your word. The same applies to gossip, as the proverb above says. But the most basic reason not to gossip is that it's just not nice. And gossip creates a toxic environment wherever it takes place — at home, at work, or anywhere else. In *Thank God It's Monday*, a great book about creating a better workplace, Roxanne Emmerich has one of the best takes on gossip that I've seen. I had always thought of gossip in the workplace as being about unseemly bits of news such as, "so-and-so is having an affair." What I hadn't understood is that gossip includes anything you say about someone else.

For example, if you have a problem with someone at work, Emmerich tells us, the right thing to do is to speak with the person with whom you have the problem, rather than discussing it with a third party. And if someone complains to you about a problem they have with a colleague, urge them to do the same. So simple. So clear. So right. Emmerich is basically telling us to be leaders.

In Chapter 2, I mentioned Don Miguel Ruiz's terrific book *The Four Agreements*. Ruiz says to avoid gossip. He explains that words are powerful and that we need to be careful with them; to speak with integrity; to say what we mean and mean what we say. Ruiz tells us to use the power of words in a positive way. This sounds like what our moms said to us when we were little (I'm repeating it because it's so important): "If you don't have anything nice to say, don't say anything at all." Mom, you were so right!

There's a great story about gossip (John Patrick Shanley incorporated this story into his play *Doubt*, which was later made into a movie) in which a woman goes to confession because she feels extremely guilty about gossiping with a friend. She asks the priest whether gossiping is a sin. The priest says that it is, and he instructs her to go home, cut open a pillow on her roof, and return to him. When she comes back, the priest asks what the result was. "Feathers everywhere, father." The priest then tells her to go back and gather up every last feather. "It can't be done," she responds. "I don't know where they went. The wind took them all over." "And that," the priest says, "is gossip."

✳ Don't Do Drugs

When my son was in high school, I liked to think that he didn't drink or use drugs. I believed him when he told me he didn't. But I could never know for sure. As a speaker told us at a parents' night at my kids' school, there are only two possible answers when you are asked whether your kids drink or use drugs: "Yes" or "I don't know."

I started talking to my kids about drinking and drugs when they were entering middle school. I then had these conversations with them, one-on-one, each year for the next few years. I occasionally brought it up with my son when I drove him home from a party, after dropping off his friends. Those seemed like good opportunities for relatively casual one-on-ones. It was always apparent from the boys' banter that they had just had a great time together. Once my son and I were alone, I would ask him whether he had had a fun night. After he told me he did, I'd ask whether he could imagine it being more fun. When he told me he couldn't, I'd say that some kids decide that they need to drink or use drugs in order to have more fun — and that besides being illegal and bad for you, it was totally unnecessary, because he couldn't possibly have more fun with his friends than he was already having. He agreed.

This strategy was my modified version of something I read when my son was about 8 years old. It was written by Doug Hall, a brilliant man who runs an incredible business called Eureka! Ranch, where I was once privileged to spend a few days brainstorming about a business my brother was starting. (At Eureka!, Doug helps people develop and commercialize innovative ideas, and he does so using techniques you would never imagine; for example, at one point we played a game with 16-sided dice to help us make decisions. You can learn more at EurekaRanch.com.) Doug wrote a piece for Universal Press Syndicate in which he told the story of Mike Salvi, who had just joined Doug's company fresh out of college. Mike told Doug that he had never experimented with drugs because of something his dad had said to him when he was about 9 years old. As Mike recounted, he had scored the game-winning basket in a youth basketball league game against one of the best teams in the league, and was carried off the court on his teammates' shoulders. He was on top of the world. Shortly after, his dad gave him a big hug and told him that the way Mike felt at that moment was called a natural high, and that drugs or alcohol weren't needed to achieve it. Over the years, Mike had found many ways to get "high on life." And during high school and college, any time he was offered drugs he would remember what his dad had told him.

✳ Leaders Delegate

In Chapter 1, I discussed how delegating can be an important step toward being happy. If you team up with other people, allowing them to do the things you don't like or are not good at, you'll be able to spend your life doing the things that you love to do and are great at. Delegation is also a critical component of being a good leader.

A large number of books have been written about leadership, many of them focusing on business leadership. Those "business books" have a lot to teach us about leadership of all kinds, and one point that they emphasize is the importance of delegating. Part of being a good leader is getting the most out of the people whom you are leading — which ultimately benefits you as well as them — and delegation is an effective way to do that. In *Leadership Jazz*, Max De Pree explains that delegation allows people to reach their potential because it gives them the opportunity to take risks and to learn by doing. As a leader, you have to know that if you delegate, mistakes may happen — it's part of the growing process for you and for the person to whom you are delegating. Monica Ramirez Basco instructs us in *Never Good Enough: Freeing Yourself From the Chains of*

Perfectionism that perfectionists need to recognize the talents of people around them and need to remember that the world won't come to an end if things don't go exactly as planned.

If you are like most people, at some time in your life you have said, "By the time I teach him how to do it, I could have done it myself." That classic line of thinking gets in the way of both progress and growth. If you follow it, you are not being a leader. If, on the other hand, we encourage the people we work with to take on new responsibilities, if we teach them new skills, it can benefit the entire group. As De Pree explains, organizations are more than one person, and a leader who limits the organization to his or her own talents seriously handicaps the group.

You have to find people who are better than you are at certain tasks. Even if you first have to train them, it will be a worthwhile investment. Yes, it's true that by the time you have shown them what to do, you could have done it yourself — once. But the next time the task needs to be done, they will be able to tackle it, freeing you up to do the things you are best at and love to do.

✳ Leaders Have Emotional Intelligence

The New York Yankees won the World Series four out of five years beginning in 1996, including three in a row from 1998–2000. Baseball fans have debated whether Joe Torre, the manager of those championship teams, was one of the greatest managers of all time or whether he was just lucky enough to lead a team filled with stars, a team with which any manager could have won. Was Torre a managing genius or not? In *The Last Night of the Yankee Dynasty,* Buster Olney, who reported on the team for the *New York Times*, writes about a telling incident from the 1999 season. The Yankees were struggling and Torre called a team meeting in Boston. He proceeded to go around the locker room giving each player just a small bit of very personal input about how they were playing. The team went on a hot streak after that meeting and went on to win the World Series that year. Reflecting on that episode, Chad Curtis, a member of the team, said that Torre had the gift of "social genius."

There are many ways to be a genius (just as there are multiple types of intelligence, as we discussed in Chapter 1), and Torre displayed a type of genius important for leaders. He exhibited what has been called "emotional intelligence." Daniel Goleman, a psychologist and former *New York Times* science reporter, wrote a book called *Emotional Intelligence* in which he describes the trait as a set of skills that includes control of one's impulses, self-motivation, empathy, and competence in interpersonal relationships. As the book's subtitle, "Why it can matter more than IQ," suggests, Goleman asserts that emotional intelligence is critical for success in life.

Torre was blessed with a group of extremely talented players. But those players were also special in ways that went beyond the statistics, such as batting average and home runs, that are traditionally used to measure baseball ability. Olney talks about the players' unselfishness, which helped each of them individually as well as the team as a whole. By thinking about their teammates, they took pressure off themselves. Torre's players, like their manager, used a lot of emotional intelligence — and some of the leadership qualities that we've discussed. You help others, and in doing so you make your own life better. (The opposite has been said of Alex Rodriguez, whose well-documented postseason struggles with the Yankees a few years later seemed directly connected to his desire to carry the team on his shoulders, and who said that he used a banned substance when he was on the Texas Rangers in response to the pressure he felt to perform as the highest-paid player on his team — and in all of baseball.)

✳ Luck Happens When Preparation Meets Opportunity

I like the saying, "Luck is what happens when preparation meets opportunity," which is attributed to the Roman philosopher Seneca. Kurt Matzler,

Franz Bailom and Todd A. Mooradian wrote in *MIT Sloan Management Review* that successful business leaders appear to possess "luck" as one of their abilities. They explained that what appears to be luck is an ability to see patterns and signals before others see them. Howard Schultz, founder of Starbucks, similarly said that what people call luck is really the ability to see things that others don't and to act on what you see. And Thomas Jefferson put it most simply when he said, "I am a great believer in luck, and I find that the harder I work, the more I have of it."

Leaders work hard and make sure they are prepared, in order to be able to take advantage of opportunities that arise. Leaders make their own luck. It's similar to the way I felt when I was writing this book. At the beginning, I did almost no research. My "research" was all the books and articles I had read over many years — books and articles I read for my own pleasure and edification — along with my life experiences and observations. Then, as I wrote, other sources, such as articles, books, and speeches, came to my attention. I often felt "lucky" to happen upon new material that would enrich the book. But I found that material because I was attuned to certain subjects as I was writing. I was no luckier than the person who is considering buying a particular type of car, and suddenly starts seeing that car "everywhere." His awareness of that car is elevated, and he starts to notice the car when he would have missed it in the past.

We've all heard the saying, "God helps those who help themselves." There's a story about a man who climbs onto his roof when a flood hits and prays for God to save him. Rescuers come by in a boat, but the man waves them off, saying, "Save someone else, God will save me." A helicopter comes by and the man waves that off, too, again saying, "Save someone else, God will save me." The flood waters rise higher and higher — and the man drowns. In heaven, he angrily asks God, "Why didn't you save me?" God answers, "I sent a boat and a helicopter. They didn't come?" Leaders help themselves. Leaders make their own luck. Be a leader.

✳ New Habits and Progress

Remember: *Life is long*, meaning we have time. If we try to make a million changes all at once, we often end up so overwhelmed that we make none. Instead, if we *slow down to make the changes*, and then *stop to celebrate the progress*, we'll accomplish much more.

Slow Down to Make the Changes — It takes 21 days to form a new habit. What are some ideas you have for new habits you would like to adopt following your reading of Chapter 3?

Stop to Celebrate the Progress — Remember to look back on all that you've accomplished. What are some areas of progress you've made?

Chapter 4
Be Organized

I talked in Chapter 1 about not sweating the small stuff, and that's an area where I work hard — but that doesn't mean I neglect details. There are many details and many tasks that we need to attend to in order to make life better.

Among all the stories I've heard of demanding rock stars, one that struck me as particularly wacky was Van Halen lead singer David Lee Roth's requirement for M&M's backstage — with all the brown ones removed. The story became much more interesting, however, when I learned that this demand was a method the band used to make sure the concert promoters had sweated all the details that were vital for a concert's success. Van Halen provided incredibly detailed and complicated instructions for their concert setups — and the M&M's requirement was buried in the middle of those instructions. If when they arrived they found brown M&M's backstage, then the band felt compelled to have every aspect of the production double-checked. Wow! That's organized!

Roth explains the M&M's trick in his memoir, *Crazy From the Heat*, and it's also recounted in *The Checklist Manifesto*, by one of my favorite writers, Dr. Atul Gawande. In the medical world, where Gawande works, patient outcomes are monitored and measured — meaning that someone is asking, "Do patients get better following surgery or another procedure?" and "How does a given doctor's or hospital's outcomes compare to others?" We all experience outcomes — results or consequences of things that happen in our lives. *The Checklist Manifesto* is Gawande's call for the use of checklists to improve outcomes in all kinds of life situations. Because I'm a big believer in checklists, his book spoke to me. The subject of this chapter, Be Organized, is about all kinds of ways to improve outcomes in our lives.

Everyone who knows me knows that I'm very organized. When I feel things getting disorganized, I become anxious. So I use to-do lists, a calendar, and many other tools to prevent things from getting disorganized. I have learned that there is no one-size-fits-all system for being organized. It's not important that you use a particular system, but it is important that you use a system — whichever one works for you. So I'm going to give you many ideas that you can adopt and combine as part of your own system.

The fact that you're reading a book like this tells me that you are more organized than most people in at least one way: You realize that you don't have to invent everything yourself, and that you can learn from the wisdom and experience of others. If you need additional help beyond the ideas in this chapter, reach out to a friend, call upon a professional organizer, or read one of the many books that deal specifically with being organized. Don't try to reinvent the wheel. Take guidance from others and put it to your own use.

✳ Write Down Everything

One of the primary ways that I stay organized is by writing down everything. When you write down everything, you never have to worry about forgetting things. I always know where I need to go (and thus I never miss appointments), I'm always on time (except for completely unavoidable situations, like getting stuck in a road closing due to a major accident), I never forget to do something that I have promised to do for someone else, and I never forget to do something that I want to do for myself. I feel so strongly about writing down everything that at one time I thought I would write a book called *Write Down Everything*.

I still frequently write down things with pen and paper. I also leave myself voicemail messages, send myself e-mails or text messages, and maintain an electronic to-do list. I write down (or type) meeting notes, always put my appointments on a calendar, keep a list of contacts, and lots more.

✳ You've Got to Know Where to Go Each Day

My dad started giving me calendars — the week-at-a-glance type in high school. He told me it was a good way to keep track of what home-work was due when, and other obligations. Nowadays, many high schools give their students such calendars (and many kids keep their calendars on smartphones).

Alan Mathog, one of my early career mentors, suggested that I buy a Franklin Day Planner organizer — a wonderful page-a-day calendar book that I used for many years before moving on to an electronic or-ganizer. Alan gave Franklin Day Planner calendars to all of his sales-people. The customer-service representatives in his office always work at the same desks, he said, but if you're a salesperson, "you've got to know where to go each day."

On my calendar, I list all my appointments — everything — personal and business appointments, as well as reminders for birthdays of family and friends. I used to be one of the only people I knew who remembered everyone's birthday. I always had a good ability to remember birthdays — but that was not my secret. My secret was that I wrote them in my calendar. Now, with computers, many more people remember birthdays, which is great.

It doesn't matter whether you keep track of things on paper or on a computer; it doesn't matter whether you use a daily, weekly, or monthly planner; and it doesn't matter whether you're working in customer service, sales, or any other area — you've got to know where to go each day.

✳ Two Secrets for Calendars

The first secret you need to know about your calendar is that you have to look at it. While that seems obvious, I've had many experiences where I was stood up for an appointment, or people were late, and afterward they said to me, "I'm so sorry. I had it on my calendar, but I forgot." Writing it on your calendar is the first step. Looking at your calendar is the critical step No. 2.

The second "secret" is to leave for appointments earlier than you have to. My dad taught me this. I always do it, and I'm never late. Traffic is a part of life almost everywhere. It's certainly a huge part of my life in the New York area. If I have an appointment in New York City at 10 am, I have to leave northern New Jersey by 8:30 am to be sure I'm on time. With no traffic, I could get there in 30 minutes. But "no traffic" is something that almost never happens, especially during rush hour. By leaving 90 minutes ahead of the meeting time, I make sure that I'll be on time. In fact, I'll be early. I learned the amount of time I needed by trial and error, and over the years I added to the amount of time as I learned how unpleasant it is to be stressed out over the possibility of being late to an appointment. These days, it's more likely that I'll leave at 8 am for that

10 am appointment. It's not that I *need* two hours to get there. But I *want* all the benefits I get when I leave early. I *want* to not be stressed, I *want* to not feel rushed, I *want* to be relaxed and at my best with whomever I'm meeting, and I *want* to not be sweating when I arrive. If I'm relaxed and feeling good, the appointment is much more likely to go well. And I'll just be in a better mood and I'll have a better day. If you do this all the time, you have more good days. If you're having more good days, you're enjoying a better life.

And being early is not just less stressful, it's also productive. When I'm early, I can plan for the appointment, review my premeeting notes (which I wrote down, of course), make phone calls, or work on other things — and with all of the technology we have these days, the sky is the limit in terms of what I can work on.

✳ Be an On-Time Person

I'm proud to be known as someone who is always on time. Harkening back to the theme of Chapter 2, showing up on time is part of being nice. Being late is inconsiderate and disrespectful. But many people are on-time-challenged. Some are so well-known for being late that their family, friends, and co-workers routinely give them an invite time earlier than they give others, so that they'll arrive at the same time as everyone else.

I have sometimes wondered whether these people just don't have a concept of time — if something in their wiring causes an inability to be on time. But a lot of those people are on time to their jobs every morning, which means that they are selective about their lateness — which points back to a lack of respect for others.

When my brother and I were in our twenties, we used to give each other rides to and from the airport when we went on trips. Many people do that for good friends. Unfortunately, my brother was always late. He was late when he was driving me — or Marcie and me — to the airport, so I would be stressed out about possibly missing my flight. He was late picking me up at the airport, so I would have to stand there waiting for him (and this was before cell phones, so I had no way of knowing where he was). It was a tough line to straddle, between appreciating the ride he was giving me and being upset about his perpetual lateness. Finally, one time after he was more than an hour late picking Marcie and me up from the airport, we lost it. We vented our frustration in a loud and angry way, which made an impression. From that day on, he was no longer late — not only for airport runs, but also for almost anything else. As anyone who knew my brother back then will attest, if you are a late person, you *can* change — you *can* become an on-time person.

I had to make a similar adjustment when it came to going out with Marcie on weekends. I like to move at a slower pace on weekends and to relax for as much time as possible before we go out, so my M.O. was to wait until the last minute to get ready, without building in as much of a cushion in the driving time as I would for business appointments during the work-week — despite the fact that I still wanted to always be on time. Then, one day, Marcie pointed out that I was getting into the bad habit of rushing on the road in order get wherever we were going on time. She said, "You see, this is where you have it all wrong. The time to rush is in the house, where we can't get into a car accident. Not on the road." She was right. I still didn't want to rush in the house, though, so I changed my habits and started getting ready earlier (and then leaving earlier) on weekends.

✳ If You're Not 10 Minutes Early, You're Late

My daughter's first high school soccer coach told the girls on their first day of practice that being on time means showing up 10 minutes early. If they were not at least 10 minutes early to practice, they would be considered late. All of my kids had already inherited the habit of being on-time people, and I was glad to see it reinforced by my daughter's coach. It's a great habit to develop.

My friend Mark used to run a car service — a company that drove people to and from airports and other places. Mark told me that his drivers followed the same rule that my daughter's soccer coach taught — if you're not at least 10 minutes early, you're late. The drivers were so good about always being early — usually much earlier than the 10-minute rule required — that Mark sometimes fielded calls from customers such as this one: "I'm calling about the car I ordered for my trip to the airport. The driver is supposed to pick us up at 9 o'clock, and I'm concerned because it's 8:30 and he's not here yet." What a wonderful, high standard they set. That's something to strive for!

✳ Time the Red Light

One way to know that you're not leaving yourself enough time is if you find yourself getting frustrated with things outside of your control, such as slow drivers and traffic lights. If that's the case, get more organized and leave earlier. You'll be a happier person. You can sit back and enjoy the ride — listening to music or talk radio, talking with your travel companion, or, if you are alone, using the time to think. That's all a lot better than being frustrated.

Something else that has helped me become more patient at traffic lights is knowing how long they last. I timed some of the lights near my house and it's good to know that a particular light, which always seems to be red when I arrive and seems to last forever, actually lasts for only one minute.

Time is a strange thing. It's amazing how fast a two-hour rock concert can fly by, and yet how long it seems to take for 60 seconds to go by when I'm waiting for my dinner to come out of the microwave. We all know how fast weekends and vacations seem to go. In *Slowing Down to the Speed of Life,* Carson and Bailey talk about how quickly the day flies by for a dentist and yet how slowly the same time goes by for the dentist's patients.

We all have the same amount of time — 24 hours each day, seven days each week. We also all experience time differently, depending on what we're doing and how we're feeling. Being organized helps us make the most of our time by minimizing the stress we feel during our daily activities.

✳ Files, Not Piles

I operate from a to-do list, not a to-do pile. If the work you have to do is in a pile in front of you, it's nearly impossible to get it all done in an effective and efficient manner. Whenever a pile starts to develop on my desk or in my in-box, I go through it. Anything I don't handle right away, I write on my to-do list, and put away in a file. An electronic to-do list is wonderful because you can easily prioritize and sort the items.

Treat e-mails just like other to-do items. If you are not going to get to certain e-mails right away, don't let them pile up in your inbox. Instead, put them in a file, an electronic file in this case, and make a note on your to-do list to get back to it.

As with your calendar, you have to look at your to-do list frequently, and it's best to check it first thing every day. I sort my list by attaching dates to each item, and then every day when I review my overall to-do list I create a priority list for that day. I never forget to do something that I promised to do on a certain date. My to-do list always has more tasks than I can get done in one day, so I'm constantly reviewing it to determine what I need to do and when — updating it, changing the action date on some items, and prioritizing based on importance and deadlines.

✳ Setting Goals

When you wake up every day, how do you know what to do first — and then what to for the rest of the day? Perhaps, like many people, you simply drag yourself out of bed, wake yourself up with a shower and some coffee, and then head to work. You spend the day working, head home, eat dinner, watch some TV, and go to sleep. Most people have days like that sometimes, and many people have days like that all the time. But you'll be happier, healthier, and more successful if you plan your days — and your life.

Being organized means having a plan — for your life, for your week, and for your day. What's the first step in having a plan? Having goals.

In the introduction, I talked a bit about setting goals. We all have goals. It's just that some of our goals are more thought out than others. For example, a person can simply exist with the goal of following the routine spelled out above — wake up, go to work, come home, watch television, go to bed. If that's good enough for you, you probably wouldn't be reading this book.

The best way to set goals is to start long term. What is it that you want to achieve in your life? Write it down. Don't agonize over this; do it quickly. You can revise it later — and you can do that as often as you would like, as your life goals become clearer over time. Set aside some time every year, if not more frequently, to write out your life goals.

Once you've written out your life goals, write down what you want to accomplish over the next five years toward achieving those goals. Then write out what you want to accomplish over the next year. Then write out what you want to accomplish this quarter. Then this week. Then, today.

It's unlikely that you'll be able to exactly stick with your life plan. But one thing is certain: You won't make even a small amount of progress on your plan if you don't *have* a plan!

In the introduction, and at the end of each chapter, I talk about the 21 days it takes to form a new habit. The goals you come up with from your life plan and your yearly plan can be broken down into 21-day habits to achieve — ways to improve your life and make your world, or the world at large, a better place. As discussed in Chapter 1, if you want to make changes to your life, the first step is to be aware of the changes you desire. If you don't have a plan, you won't create the awareness you need to make changes in your life.

Just thinking about your future helps you to have a better future. Richard E. Nisbett, a professor at the University of Michigan, cited an example of this phenomenon (in a *New York Times* Op-Ed piece) when he wrote about Daphna Oyserman, a social psychologist at the University of Michigan who asked inner-city junior-high-school children in Detroit a series of questions about the kind of future they would like to have and how they might handle difficulties that arose. The children who went through these life-planning exercises showed improved performance on standardized academic tests, and their failure rate was reduced by more than half.

❋ Time Management

There are more books, theories, and philosophies on time management than on almost any other topic in the personal development genre. A search of Amazon.com, for example, yielded 1,700 hits.

For many people, the biggest time-management challenge is making time for the most important things — those things that you identify when you set your goals. The problem is that we all get buried in a mountain of e-mails, calls, and other to-do items that require our immediate attention on a daily basis. If we don't make time for the bigger, more important things, we will often never get to them, imperiling not only our productivity, but also our health and our happiness.

If a person running a company spent all his or her time answering the phone and responding to e-mails, he or she wouldn't have time for developing new business ideas. But that's a perfect example of how many of us often behave: We are aware of important things we should be doing, but we put them off because we are overwhelmed by all the pressing items on our to-do list. The solution? Schedule time for the things that are important, but that do not require your immediate attention. Write it down on your calendar. And then do it.

Stephen Covey has terrific ideas on the subject of time management. He provides a great time-management tool in his books, and check out his big rocks story in *The 7 Habits of Highly Effective Families* or listen to it on Covey's cassette version of *The 7 Habits of Highly Effective People.* I saw an animated version of the story, and when I showed it to one of my daughters when she was 11 years old, she said, "If I'm ever a teacher, I'm going to show that to my students."

Exercise is a good example of an activity that you need to be sure to schedule. If you don't exercise on a given day, it won't cause an immediate problem (although may not feel as good that day as you would if you had exercised), and only you will know that you skipped the workout. But exercise is important — extremely important. If you don't make exercise a priority, it will *become* your No. 1 priority when a doctor tells you that you will have serious health problems, and might die prematurely, if you don't get more physically active. As Clayton M. Chrtistensen, Jerome Grossman, and Jason Hwang write in their book, *The Innovator's Prescription*, the majority of people make their health a priority only after they become sick. Or as my friend Abe says, "If we spend all our time building our wealth, we'll soon enough be spending all our wealth fixing our health." We'll talk more about this in Chapter 6, Be Healthy.

Doing things right the first time is another good example of something you have to create time for, even if it doesn't seem urgent at that moment. As someone in the construction business said to me, "How come we never seem to have enough time to do it right the first time, but we always have enough time to do it over?" You've been there, haven't you? You don't put in the time to do something exactly right, and then you end up having to put in even more time later, when you have to fix your mistake.

✳ Haste Makes Waste

I bet your mother, like mine, told you that "haste makes waste." When I was a boy, I didn't pay this lesson much heed. Now, I'm a big believer. I tell myself those three words all the time, reminding myself to slow down and do things right the first time. For example, it's been extremely important for me to make sure I don't hurt myself by lifting things that are too heavy or cumbersome. You might be tempted to try moving a heavy object yourself in an effort to get it done quickly, but you can do permanent damage to yourself if you're not careful — like if you lift something improperly, bending your back instead of bending your knees. I did that many times when I was younger, and I'm paying the price today with chronic back issues.

The "haste makes waste" mantra has also helped me in other ways. When I was a kid, my room was always a mess. As is the case with many kids (including my own), my room tended to look like a tornado had just passed through. I figured I would be like that forever. But when I became a grown-up, I realized that it's much easier to take a few extra seconds to put everything where it belongs. I'm not a neat freak. My closet isn't very neat. The clothes are not perfectly folded, and the piles aren't straight.

But I am kind of an organization freak. I like to have everything in its place because it's frustrating when I can't find something and I have to *waste* time looking for it. Less frustration = a better life.

Another "haste makes waste" example is my handwriting, which has always been terrible. To this day, my most vivid memories of my elementary-school education are of being yelled at by my teachers for my scribbling. (And those incidents are memorable for my elementary-school classmates as well, as I learned when one of them, Calvin Cauthen, said to me at our 10-year high school reunion, and again at our 20th: "David Singer…How's your penmanship?") My handwriting is so bad sometimes that I can't even read it myself. I'll scribble a couple of words as a reminder to do something, and later I'll stare at the note, unable to decipher it. I've had to work hard to remember to take a few extra seconds to write neatly enough so that later I can read what I wrote and remember what it is that I'm supposed to remember.

✳ Eat the Big Frog First

Imagine you need to eat three live frogs. One is small, the second is medium, and the third is large. If you eat the smallest first, it's bound to be such a revolting experience that the idea of eating the medium frog (and even worse, the large frog) is going to be so objectionable that you won't be able to proceed. On the other hand, if you eat the big frog first, the medium frog won't seem like such a big deal. And the small frog will seem like nothing.

I first heard about "eating the big frog first" in the mid-1990s from a gentleman named Danny Cox, who spoke at a business conference I attended. It's a great way to help you avoid procrastinating about the things on your to-do list.

Although I'm good at prioritizing, my to-do list often falls victim to my fears. Certain items feel harder or scarier or less appealing to me. The bottom line is I need to work extra hard sometimes to make sure I do the most important things first. I look at my list at the beginning of each day and say to myself, "Eat the big frog first" — do the thing after which everything else on the list will seem easy. We all have things that for some reason we don't want to do — things we're nervous about doing and are likely to procrastinate about. I find when I do those things first, it gives me an extra great feeling of accomplishment, which is a terrific way to start my day.

Procrastination *can* serve a purpose: If you're truly not ready to do a task; if you haven't convinced yourself to be confident about tackling it, it may be better to put it off. But usually, delaying it just causes more dread and unpleasantness. As Danny Cox explained when I first learned about eating the big frog, prolonging painful experiences is not something we normally choose to do. Kids don't slowly sip cough syrup — they gulp it down fast to get it over with. And we don't slowly pull off a bandage, we rip it off. My mother-in-law, who never procrastinates, puts it this way: "Procrastination makes everything doubly hard — you not only have to do it, you also have to think about doing it." Similarly, William James said, "There's nothing so fatiguing as an uncompleted task."

Whether "eating the big frog first" helps you or not, be sure you do the most important things first each day.

✳ Don't Leave Your E-mail Open All the Time

To stop e-mail from controlling your day, pick certain times of the day to look at it. My most productive days are the ones where I have appointments all day and only check my e-mail at the end of the day. Some jobs require you to check e-mail more frequently. In that case, read one of the books that have been written about controlling e-mail's impact on your time management. I recommend, for example, *Never Check E-Mail In the Morning*, by professional organizing guru Julie Morgenstern.

✳ Consider Hiring a Professional Organizer

I know a lot about professional organizers because my wife is one. Professional organizers spend time with people at their homes and/or offices learning about their organizational needs and challenges, and help them develop systems that will make their lives less stressful. Treating her work with a doctor/patient-like confidentiality, Marcie never tells me about the people she works with. But, from my own experience, and from reading about the work that professional organizers do, I know that there are many people out there who need a little help, and many who need a lot. For example, I've read articles about people who have houses full of what other people would consider to be clutter, junk, or even garbage: a decade's worth of newspapers, clothing that they no longer use, and — a very common problem — piles of papers all over the place. Professional organizers help to organize one's "stuff," which can include sorting things, finding places for what needs to be kept, throwing out a lot, and selling or donating items.

Early on in Marcie's career as a professional organizer I realized why she was so good at what she does: She customizes solutions for each client. What I mean by that is best illustrated by its opposite — what I would do. I am arguably even more organized than Marcie. And if you let me into your house, I would be able to quickly organize it. The problem is that it would be organized in a way that works for me, but not necessarily for you. Chances are you would lapse back into your old ways soon after I left. Conversely, when a good professional organizer prescribes a solution, it's one that is customized to the client's needs. "I don't organize people," Marcie says. "I organize their lives."

You can find a professional organizer at napo.net, the Web site of the National Association of Professional Organizers. NAPO's brochure lists the benefits of a professional organizer for your home:

> Bring order, calm, and control to your home and family life.
>
> Save money by organizing your bills, your shopping, and your clothing.
>
> Get more done in less time.
>
> Put your house in order so you can find what you need…

All of this also applies to work environments. My company has hired professional organizers to help some of the people in our office to be more organized.

✳ Saving Money — Coupons

Being organized can help you save money in many ways. For example, you have to be organized to use coupons. You have to collect the coupons, know when they expire, and use them. You shouldn't buy things just because you have a coupon, but use coupons for things you otherwise would buy at full price. Individual coupons are not big money, but they are free money. Many people wouldn't bend down to pick up a penny on the street. But most would stop to pick up two quarters. So why not use a 50-cent coupon? And if it's "double coupons week" at your supermarket, the 50-cent coupon is like finding a dollar. Coupons are worthless, though, if you can't remember where you put then, or if they sit in a pile of papers until they expire.

✳ Saving Money and Time — Buying in Bulk

Buying in bulk is a way to be organized in your shopping; it saves money, and it makes a lot of sense. When there is a sale on nonperishable items you would buy anyway, why not stock up? For example, when my local supermarket has a buy-one-get-one-free sale on the brand of almonds that I like, I buy enough to last me for a while. The cans have a "best before" date on the bottom that is usually about two years away. Because I eat about a can a week, the almonds are gone long before that.

Sometimes buying in bulk is the smart thing to do even if things aren't on sale. It's a huge waste of time to keep going back to the supermarket to buy the same things. I try to minimize the number of trips. Why should I buy one or two boxes of cereal each time I go to the store? It's much more efficient to buy many boxes — as long as you know when the expiration dates are. In the case of cereal, that's usually many months away. I even buy milk in bulk. The milk we like has a "sell by" date that is weeks, or even a month away, and we go through about a half gallon every two days.

I similarly buy apples in quantity. They last quite a while when they're in the fridge, and I like them better cold and crisp anyway. And when the half-gallon containers of orange juice are on sale, I'll buy four (as long as the expiration date is far enough away). I also buy lightbulbs and HVAC filters in bulk. Why should I go to the store each time I need a new one?

It's particularly helpful to buy in bulk if you're shopping at a store that isn't nearby. For example, because Marcie and I buy a lot of things at Trader Joe's, which is a bit of a drive from our house, we stock up there. In an admittedly extreme example of organizing, I created a Trader Joe's buying sheet, to which I stapled cereal box tops and other food labels. I know this is one of the more unusual actions I have told you about. When I gave it to Marcie, I thought she would give me a "you've really gone off the deep end this time" look. I was wrong. She loved it. She occasionally stops at Trader Joe's if she happens to be passing it, but she was tired of coming home with her full shopping bags, happy about her purchases, only to find out that she bought a cereal that none of us likes because it looked so similar to the ones we usually get.

✳ Bulk Wine

When I find an inexpensive bottle of wine I like, I buy a bunch. I'm not an expert on wine. I rarely find a bottle that I hate, but I also rarely find one that I love. When I do find one I particularly like, and the person in the store tells me it will last a long time (or will even get better with age), I'll buy six or more bottles, which I can use when people come over, when we need to bring a bottle to someone's house, or when we go to a BYOB (bring your own bottle) restaurant — which is another good way to save money because it's much less costly to bring your own bottle.

✳ I Even Buy Clothing in Bulk

When I find an item of clothing I like, I often buy two or more. (The definition of "like" means I like how it looks and feels, and I like its price.) There is a bit of a risk with the way fashions change, but I rarely have been burned because my tastes are simple.

I also try to be organized and prepared when I head out to shop. I know what I want to buy when I go clothing shopping — this way, when I see the thing that I want, at a good price, I snap it up.

One caveat about bulk buying: You need room to store things. Marcie and I keep the extra cereal in the basement, and we keep milk in an old fridge in our garage. But however large your home is, you'll have more storage space if you're organized. And with more storage space, you can save more money.

✳ Don't Waste Food

Being organized means not throwing away food unless you absolutely have to. It's wasteful when you throw away food. In addition to what your mom used to say about remembering those poor people starving in some far-off land, which is true (and they're starving in America as well), throwing away food is also a waste of money. When you cook a meal, save the leftovers in the fridge for a specific upcoming meal — whether it's tomorrow's lunch or tomorrow's dinner. Marcie has a really good system for the kids' lunches: As soon as we get up from dinner, but before all the food is put away, the kids put together their lunches from dinner. If you want to save food for longer than that, freeze it — but label it with a date and an indication of what it is (because it can be hard to identify some things after they've gotten frosty in the freezer). It's a lot of effort to prepare meals, and if you are organized about it you can make the experience more productive, which will save you money *and* time. We almost always have leftovers because we intentionally cook more than we need and freeze it — we usually double or triple every recipe we make.

✳ Date Everything

Labeling things with dates is a critical part of being organized. Every note I write to someone has a date on it. Every document I create is dated. The dates help you sort things. And they create a historical record. They allow you to look back and see how things developed over time. I like how e-mails automatically have dates on them, so you can track the progression of conversations.

✳ Don't Reinvent the Wheel

Another reason I write down everything is that I hate reinventing the wheel. I find it frustrating to do the same things over and over, each time starting from scratch. In order to avoid that, here are some of the things I write down:

In my contact list, in addition to phone numbers, I note phone extensions where applicable, so that I can dial them directly rather than repeatedly having to use a dial-by-name system.

When Marcie and I travel, I keep notes of what we do on the trip. This way, if we go back to the same place (as we have done on several occasions), we can hit the high spots and avoid repeating mistakes. If I don't write down everything, it would be hard years later to recall what worked and what didn't. I've also shared my notes with friends when they've asked for information about where we stayed, where we ate, and what to avoid.

At my office, there are numerous procedures that we put in writing. Though our company is not a franchisor, the company's growth has benefited from one of the secrets of franchising: We compile strategies and methods that have been successful, so that others can replicate the success without having to figure everything out anew.

I have a list of the wattages of all ceiling (and other hard-to-reach) lightbulbs in our house. Why? Because it saves a step when a bulb needs to be changed. Instead of climbing up to unscrew the bulb, reading its wattage, getting a new lightbulb, and then climbing up again to screw in the new one, I bring the replacement bulb with me on the first climb.

I have a list of what I pack for vacations and a different list for business trips. Otherwise, I forget vitamins or exercise sneakers or something else.

I keep a list of all the restaurants I go to. If I loved a restaurant, I want to go back; if I didn't like it, I don't want to. Sometimes it's hard for me to remember. So I write it down. And if I loved or disliked a certain dish, I write that down, too.

Marcie and I keep a list of gift ideas for our kids. I keep a list of gift ideas for her.

When our kids were young, we often struggled to find things to do with them. So we made a list and kept adding to it, and referred to it when we were at a loss for ideas.

When we used to go rent movies at the store, we never seemed to be able to find one we wanted to see, despite having hundreds to choose from. So I started keeping a list of movies we wanted to see — kind of my own Netflix list before Netflix.

Before we had the Internet and GPS devices, I used to save directions to friends' and relatives' homes, beaches, and other places I knew we would visit again and again. For a few places I still use those old directions because they seem to be better than the ones on the Internet map services. I also save some other information about driving trips, such as the best times to go to certain beaches to avoid traffic.

When Marcie at one point got frustrated that the kids never seemed to like what she prepared for dinner, I began compiling a list of the things they liked to eat. A few weeks later, when she was about to make dinner but was already feeling frustrated in the expectation that the kids were going to reject the food, I presented her with the list. I subsequently did the same thing with snack ideas, because we were struggling to think of a variety of healthful snacks to have on hand when the kids came home from school. Marcie expanded my dinner ideas list into a recipe binder. She also has a wardrobe binder — in effect, a set of clothing "recipes" that she can review when deciding on an outfit.

If all of this seems like a bit much, consider this story about Albert Einstein: When a reporter once asked for his phone number, Einstein grabbed a phone book to look it up. The reporter was baffled that the renowned genius didn't know his own phone number, and said so to Einstein. Einstein reportedly responded something to the effect of, "Why should I memorize something when I know where to look it up?"

Maybe your memory is better than mine (and Einstein's) and you think it's unnecessary to write down everything. It just seems to me that we all have so many things to remember, so much information cluttering our minds, that the more we can write down and forget about until we need it, the better we can devote our brainpower and energy to the most important things.

✳ Ask Yourself, "Am I Being Organized?"

In the movie *Dirty Harry*, Clint Eastwood's Harry Callahan character famously challenges a crook, telling him to ask himself one question: "Do I feel lucky?"

My message to you is that you've got to ask yourself one question: Do I feel organized? Because if you don't, you're probably just hoping that you'll be lucky, hoping that things will work out for you without doing everything you should be doing to put the odds in your favor. At the end of the previous chapter I said that leaders make their own luck. One way they do that is by being organized. Be organized.

✳ New Habits and Progress

Remember: *Life is long,* meaning we have time. If we try to make a million changes all at once, we often end up so overwhelmed that we make none. Instead, if we *slow down to make the changes,* and then *stop to celebrate the progress,* we'll accomplish much more.

Slow Down to Make the Changes — It takes 21 days to form a new habit. What are some ideas you have for new habits you would like to adopt following your reading of Chapter 4?

Stop to Celebrate the Progress — Remember to look back on all that you've accomplished. What are some areas of progress you've made?

Chapter 5

Be a Lifelong Learner

Legendary psychologist Abraham Maslow said that humans have an instinctual need to make the most of their abilities and to strive to be the best they can be. By this point in the book, it's pretty obvious that I follow that instinct. I constantly work to improve myself, and this book is a product of my lifelong learning — what I have learned from other people, from reading, and from experiences I've had. Walter Breuning, who was the world's oldest man when he died in 2011 at the age of 114, said in an interview in *Men's Journal* shortly before his death, that the key to his long life (in addition to eating well and exercising, which we'll discuss in the next chapter), was keeping his mind operating at all times. And Henry Ford said, "Anyone who stops learning is old, whether at 20 or 80." The importance of keeping one's brain young should be enough of an impetus for us to be lifelong learners. If you haven't made the time for learning (or haven't made an effort to learn from your experiences), I urge you to do so. I hope you'll be inspired by this chapter to find new habits you can adopt to become a lifelong learner, an important piece of a having a better life.

✳ Classroom Learning

In the late 1980s, a few years after I graduated from college, I had an itch to take classes again. I enrolled in the adult-education program at a local high school, where I took two semesters of tai chi. Fancying myself an aspiring novelist, I took a creative-writing class through The Learning Annex. That adult-education organization had just gotten its start in 1980, and the boxes containing their brochures were ubiquitous on Manhattan street corners at that time. When I went through a brief "aspiring real estate mogul" phase, I took a real estate class there as well. Later, I decided to learn how to get rich in the stock market and took a class on investments. While I didn't go into any of these professions, in all three cases the learning was worthwhile.

✳ Reading

I'm a huge advocate of learning by reading. I've learned a ton by reading. In addition to the personal growth I've experienced from reading "self-help"-type books (finding new habits to adopt to help me to become a happier, healthier, and better person, as I've documented in this book), I've learned a lot about selling, marketing, management, leadership, and other business topics, and I've learned about my most important job — parenting — which I'll talk about later in this chapter. I also love learning about things that can help others. I recommend books to people all the time. I send them links to articles and blogs. And I share articles with the whole world on Twitter *@sixsimplerules*. If you're an avid reader already, perhaps this section will give you some ideas for helping others with their reading.

You often hear readers say that reading takes them places they couldn't otherwise go. I've certainly had that experience and it's incredibly enriching. Yet my love of reading didn't come to me until I was a grown-up. In high school, I hated the classics we were assigned to read and often read the *Cliff's Notes* versions rather than the books. Reading books just didn't do it for me. Many years later, as a parent, I frequently heard about the importance of reading to kids from the earliest age. I read with my children as often as I could, and my parents did the same with me. I clearly remember my parents reading to me (and later I did the reading while I sat with them) from *Where the Wild Things Are*, *The Story About Ping* (about a duck who gets lost on the Yangtze River), and the various *Curious George* books.

Somehow, for me, that early childhood love of books did not translate into a love of reading in adolescence. In high school I only read the sports pages in the newspaper every morning (which I still do today); *Sports Illustrated* magazine, which I enjoyed more for the photos than anything else; and the books assigned for classes (which, as I said, I often skipped in favor of *Cliff's Notes*). Other than that, I read nothing.

In college I quickly learned that there were no shortcuts. Freshman year was a huge wake-up call for me. I wasn't prepared for the volume of work. There was no way I was going to pass Economics 101, or any other class, without reading the textbook. In high school I had coasted and gotten B's. In college, coasting would have resulting in flunking. I had to work hard to get B's (a sort of minimum standard I had set for myself during high school). Then I had some good fortune academically. You hear about kids falling in with a "bad crowd." I fell in with a good crowd. My freshman-year girlfriend's roommate was smart, and a hard worker. Her boyfriend was as well. The two of them were actually competitive with each other, and their competitiveness rubbed off on me. For the first time since elementary school, I found myself wanting to get A's. And I did. I got many A's during the rest of my years in college, and in working hard to get those A's, I learned a lot. I also expanded my interests. I was a business major with a minor in computer science, but in my junior year I decided to also minor in English — something that would have been unfathomable to me when I was in high school. I sought out great professors as I became a better student. I worked harder, was more achievement oriented, and read what I was supposed to read, from Shakespeare to science fiction — and I enjoyed it.

But, after college, I fell back to not reading.

Again, I was fortunate, when a couple of years after college I fell in with another good crowd. Specifically, I became friends with Alan Mathog (whom I discussed in Chapter 4). Alan loved to read, and read constantly. He also regularly gave gifts of books that he had enjoyed, particularly books on personal and professional development. My limited reading was evident when I visited Alan's office after my honeymoon. He asked me what I had read on the trip. I told him I read baseball player Dave Winfield's biography (*Winfield: A Player's Life*). "That's it?" he asked incredulously.

As the entrepreneurial part of my career took off, I began to enjoy the business books recommended to me by Alan and others. I loved how much I was learning from reading. Even if I didn't directly learn something from a particular book, its ideas would stimulate thinking that would motivate me and lead me to new ideas.

But, as I explained in this book's introduction, on nonwork days I only read for pleasure — no business books, no trade journals, no work-related articles. As I learned from Dan Sullivan, days off are truly rejuvenating only if you completely escape work. My dad always told me to make sure to take days off, to go on vacations, and to not call the office (or, these days, check e-mail) when I'm away from work. He had it almost totally right. You have to go all the way and not even read anything related to work.

Once I discovered the importance of complete escape from work, and the rejuvenation it brings, I started to catch up on all the nonbusiness books I had never read, and that turned me into a voracious reader. I developed a love for the works of certain popular authors, reading everything written by Clive Cussler, Ken Follett, John Sandford, Michael Connelly, Michael Crichton, Nelson DeMille, John Irving, John Grisham, Pat Conroy, Nick Hornby, and others. Then I accidentally stumbled on *Summer of '49*, by David Halberstam, a wonderful book about the dramatic pennant race between the New York Yankees and the Boston Red Sox during the 1949 baseball season. I became addicted to nonfiction, especially biographies of sports figures, civil rights leaders, and presidents, to the point that fiction seemed unimportant to me. Eventually I returned to fiction and started alternating between fiction and nonfiction. But this time around I was reading classics, such as the books of Edith Wharton and Jane Austen. And on work days I continued to read business and personal development books.

Through reading, I've not only learned a tremendous amount, but I've also become a much more well-rounded (and probably more interesting) person. Often I read more than one book at the same time, a fiction book and a nonfiction book — it's hard for me to keep the characters straight if I read two works of fiction simultaneously. I finish one book every week or two and much more when I'm on vacation (Alan Mathog will be proud of me when he reads this).

How do I fit in all that reading? I read while exercising.

In the beginning of my exercising days, I watched TV while working out. Now, I prefer reading to watching TV while I exercise (and in other situations where I have a choice; on planes, for example, I almost always read rather than watch the movie). I read about a page every minute or two. That means that I read 15-30 pages a day if I exercise for 30 minutes (and I often exercise for longer than 30 minutes). I also read at other times during the day, if possible. When you do the math, you can see how I read a book each week or two. Even if you read more slowly than I do, you can read a lot. If you read 10 pages a day, you should be able to read a book every month, which means in three years you'll have read 36 books. That's pretty awesome. I'll talk more about reading while exercising in Chapter 6, Be Healthy.

Like most readers, I'm opportunistic about my reading. I frequently carry a book with me on errands where I might be kept waiting (such as a doctor's appointment), and when I'm traveling I bring along more reading than I could ever finish. Digital readers allow you to carry tons of reading in one small device, although for now I still like paper.

✳ Finding Books

There are a variety of ways in which I learn about books I want to read. Often it comes from word of mouth. Readers love to tell people — especially other readers — about books they've enjoyed. And when I love a book, in addition to telling others about it I immediately look for additional books by the same author. Earlier I mentioned some of the fiction writers whose books I've read. I've similarly read all the works of nonfiction writers such as David Halberstam, David McCullough, Michael Lewis, David Sedaris, Dave Eggers, Bill Bryson, and John Feinstein.

As for personal development books, I've discussed many of them throughout this book. My two favorite authors are Richard Carlson and Stephen Covey. I was so awed by Carlson's *Don't Sweat the Small Stuff* that I went out and bought a book he co-authored, *Slowing Down to the Speed of Life*, which was even more powerful for me. And I've read nearly every book by Covey. My favorite is *The 7 Habits of Highly Effective Families*, which I found easier to understand and relate to than the original classic, *The 7 Habits of Highly Effective People*. Many personal development writers refer to those who have influenced their thinking — as I've done in this book — and such references by Covey and others led me to numerous other books that have enriched my life.

I peruse the book reviews that appear in the *New York Times* and the *Wall Street Journal* to learn about new books I might wish to read, and I like to look at the *Times* critics' lists of the top books of the year. I also look to see which books win the Pulitzer Prizes and National Book Awards each year.

Quite a few "best books of the century" lists were published just before and after the year 2000, and those lists are great sources of reading recommendations. I'd like to someday read all the books on the Modern Library's 100 Best Novels list (so far I've read very few of them). The Modern Library has other lists as well, including the best nonfiction of the 20th century. I've read most of the books on *Sports Illustrated*'s Top 100 Sports Books of All Time.

There are so many books out there. No one has time to read every one, so, as with everything in life, we have to make choices. If I don't like a book, I put it down. But usually I'll read quite a few pages before doing that because some of the best books I've read did not grab me initially.

✳ Books to Help Me With My Most Important Job — Parenting

My most important and meaningful job over the past couple of decades has been my job as a dad, and I've read many parenting books. Here are glowing reviews of some of my favorites:

1-2-3 Magic: Effective Discipline for Children 2-12, by Thomas W. Phelan. This brilliant book helped me to get past the common predicament of being too "nice" to follow through on threatened punishments for my pouting children. I learned that I was making a big mistake in how I was communicating with them. As the authors write, reasoning with your children isn't always effective:

Imagine your 8-year-old is torturing his little sister for the 40th time that day. You ask him how he would feel if someone did that to him. He says, "You know, you're right, I wouldn't like it very much. How insensitive I've been," and he stops — permanently. How nice, but it just doesn't happen in real life.

The book goes on to provide tactics that actually work to change children's behavior. This is the book that helped me stop yelling at my young children and taught me to use a more effective and pleasant way of disciplining them. And the book lived up to its title — the author's method worked like magic.

Protecting the Gift: Keeping Children and Teenagers Safe (and Parents Sane), by Gavin de Becker. This book's title communicates how worthwhile it is. De Becker is a security expert. He taught me that fear is a gift that must be acted upon. Fear allows us to have the intuition to protect ourselves and our children. We need to trust our intuition. When we feel that there is an unsafe situation, we must speak out about it or we will worry. If we speak out about it, we may offend somebody, but we will have protected our children, and we won't worry anymore (the "keeping parents sane" part of the title).

When my son, Jeremy, was 7, he came home one day and told Marcie and me that he and a friend had been playing with the friend's BB gun. I felt it wasn't safe. If I hadn't read *Protecting the Gift*, I might have felt uncomfortable confronting the situation. Instead, I told my son's friend's parents that I wasn't comfortable with the kids playing with a BB gun and that if they couldn't assure me that it wouldn't happen again, I wouldn't let Jeremy go to their house.

Another time, I felt empowered to speak with a friend who had briefly left her son and Jeremy at home with just their older daughter, who was only 10. My friend told me that I worried too much. I explained that the opposite was true — that if I were to let Jeremy stay with the 10-year-old, I would worry, but that by speaking up I was avoiding having to worry.

We often fear that we are not being nice if we tell other people about our concerns; we think that we'll offend or insult the other person, and we're embarrassed to speak up about how we feel. But after reading de Becker's book, I stopped letting the fear of embarrassment interfere with my most important priorities.

De Becker is so smart and has so much to offer. Please read his book.

(On a similar subject, please also find resources to learn about the dangers of online predators so that you can effectively protect your children.)

Get Out of My Life, but First Could You Drive Me & Cheryl to the Mall: A Parent's Guide to the New Teenager, by Anthony E. Wolf, PhD. With this book (as with *Men Are From Mars, Women Are From Venus,* which I discussed in Chapter 2), I felt as if the author must have lived in our house. Those kinds of books blow my mind. When Jeremy was in ninth grade, and particularly after he started having girlfriends, Marcie felt a great loss. Jeremy wouldn't hug her anymore. He wouldn't talk to her. Everything we were going through with Jeremy was covered in *Get Out of My Life,* which was extremely helpful. The book taught us, among many other things, that what was going on in our house was normal and typical — that numerous moms and teenage sons go through what Marcie and Jeremy were going through. And as the book predicted, it was just a phase. Jeremy "came back" a couple of years later.

When you think about how much you learn from books, you realize what a great deal they are. A hardcover book may be more expensive than a movie ticket, but in terms of cost per hour, reading the book is actually cheaper than seeing the movie. And you get to keep the book forever and you can refer to it over and over again. The value you get from a personal development book is far greater than the amount you spend on it. Even if you get just one good idea from a book, it's worth the investment. That's why I never hesitate to buy books that I think will help me.

✳ Reading in Addition to Books

I read quite a bit in addition to books. I read the *New York Times* and the *Wall Street Journal* every day. I also read a New Jersey newspaper, the *Record*, which I have been reading since I was a kid, when it was called the *Bergen Record* (as in Bergen County, New Jersey). As a boy, I occasionally delivered the *Bergen Record* when Jimmy, our paperboy, was away.

I don't attempt to read three newspapers each day cover to cover. For each paper, I tend to read headlines and the occasional articles that catch my interest. I read many articles in the sports pages and a lot of Op-Ed pieces. Simply looking at headlines keeps me abreast of the general go-ings-on in the world. The *Record* has comics — I read *Dilbert* and then leave the comics page folded open for my kids. The *New York Times* has a famous crossword puzzle, which I'll talk about later.

I usually read the newspapers over breakfast. Some people say that if you are doing something else while you're eating, you aren't paying atten-tion to what you're eating, you aren't truly enjoying your food, and as a result, you're probably eating too much. I've worked hard to remember to eat slowly and savor my food, and I know I'm compromising by using breakfast time to read the morning papers, but I just like it a lot better than reading the back of the cereal box over and over.

Over the years I've subscribed to many different magazines, but usually no more than two or three at a time. I like *Prevention* and I receive e-mails that link to blogs and articles on health and wellness topics from Dr. Andrew Weil, WebMD®, Rodale (*Prevention's* publisher), RealAge®, and several other Web sites on living a balanced life, most of which I learned about through the use of Twitter.

I enjoy the online or print version of the satirical newspaper *The Onion*. (Laughter is wonderful for many reasons, including that it's good for your happiness and health. I recommend that you find ways to laugh as often as you can. I love reading funny books and wish I could find more of them.) I also read several business and trade magazines we subscribe to at our office. To reduce the burden on each of us, we circulate each magazine only after someone we have designated as that magazine's "primary reader" has gone through the issue first, marking articles for specific people — or for everyone — to read.

✳ Brain Food/Brain Exercise

My mother-in-law (age 86 as this book goes to print) has traded books with me for many years, and I know that she reads both for pleasure and to keep her brain young. Exercising your brain — through reading or activities such as games and puzzles — is strongly recommended to help keep you young.

I've become a huge fan of puzzles. In the summer of 2005, Marcie and I were spending a day with our niece, Tracie, who was 24 at the time. Tracie was working at CBS on *The Morning Show* and she seemed to know about all the newest trends. "Uncle David, you have to try this new puzzle, Sudoku," she said to me on that beautiful afternoon. We were sitting by my aunt's pool and Tracie had brought a book of Sudoku puzzles. She explained to me that the *New York Post* had been publishing Sudoku, a type of puzzle that had caused a huge sensation in Japan, and that Sudoku's popularity was quickly soaring in New York. She taught me how to do it and off I ran. I had always been a "math person" as a kid, and this puzzle appealed to my interest in numbers and logic. I picked up a *New York Post* Sudoku book that week and started to do the puzzles regularly. That fall, the *Record* began to publish Sudoku, with an "easy" puzzle on Monday, and progressively harder puzzles each day through Saturday. I began doing that puzzle every day, and it took me nearly a year before I was able to finish a Saturday puzzle. Over the course of that year I was also given a bunch of Sudoku books as presents.

A couple of years later I discovered crossword puzzles. It's hard to live in the New York area your whole life and not be familiar with the *New York Times* crossword puzzle. All you have to do is to spend some time on the city's subways, or on the commuter trains or buses to the suburbs, and you will see many of the puzzle's devotees. There was even a documentary film made in 2006 about the *Times'* longtime puzzle editor Will Shortz and his fans. I saw the movie (it's called *Wordplay* and I recommend it), I often saw my mom and aunt doing the puzzle, for years I watched commuters filling it out on the train, and I passed the puzzle in the pages of the *Times* thousands of times, but until September of 2008 I had tried the puzzle only once — and I had quickly put it down when I realized I was way out of my league. Then, one Sunday afternoon Marcie and I were at a friend's house and two people were enthusiastically talking about the *New York Times* crossword puzzle. I decided to give it a try the next day. To my amazement, I completed the puzzle. As with Sudoku, the puzzles get harder each day of the week, and when I tried it on Tuesday it was significantly more challenging — but with some perseverance, I got it done. I was unable to complete Wednesday's and could barely begin Thursday's. For the next few weeks, I followed that pattern. I figured I would get better at it, and I did. But I was a bit impatient with my progress, and I wasn't enjoying the days after Tuesday

— I wasn't even enjoying the Tuesday puzzles that much. So I bought myself a bunch of books full of past Monday puzzles. They were fun and challenging, but I was able to complete most of them. After about a year, I started to do the Tuesday puzzle in the *Times* each week and now I can usually complete that one as well. (And because I don't commute by train or bus, I often don't do the puzzle on the day it's published, so two a week is a good number for me anyway.)

I recall being told long ago that if I had been a bigger reader as a kid, I would have done better on the English portion of the SAT exam. That's probably true, because all these years later, after reading hundreds of books, I find the SAT English section very doable. (When my kids went through the SAT age, Marcie and I both tried many practice questions.) And I know that if I had tried the *Times* crossword puzzle back in high school or college, even on a Monday, I wouldn't have done as well as I do today.

In early 2009, the *Times* began to publish another Japanese numbers puzzle, KenKen. I enjoyed learning KenKen and the additional math element that it contains. I mastered it far more quickly than I did Sudoku. If you haven't tried KenKen, check it out. It's a lot of fun.

✳ The Importance of Coaches — Not Just for Athletes

I've enjoyed the privilege of having many coaches. My first coaches were my parents. I've talked about Alan Mathog, the wonderful mentor and coach from the early part of my career. I've talked about the Strategic Coach® Program. The name tells you right away why I mention it here. I'm grateful for all that I've learned from my participation in the program — Dan Sullivan and many members of his team have been incredible coaches for me, personally and professionally.

I've also learned a tremendous amount from therapists. We've come a long way, but for some people there is still a bit of a stigma attached to going to a psychiatrist, psychologist, social worker, analyst, or anyone similar. Like so many other people you can learn from, these professionals can be a great part of your learning. If it makes you feel better, think of them as life coaches. In the next chapter, Be Healthy, I talk a bit more about the importance of embracing the concept of life coaches. For now, I want to say: 1) Marcie and I went to a life coach who helped us with relationship and parenting issues when we were dealing with the stresses of having three kids under 5; 2) Marcie and I went again about 10 years later when we were dealing with the stresses of having three teens; and 3) I have benefited from individual time with life coaches. I love it. It's like a book — only better because it's an interactive experience. Professional athletes use coaches. Roger Federer, arguably the greatest tennis player ever, has a coach. Michael Jordan, arguably the greatest basketball player ever, had a coach. I figure if they can keep learning from coaches and improving their skills, even when they're the best at what they do, so can I.

✳ Public Speaking

I have a bunch of public-speaking coaches as a member of an organization called Toastmasters. As the Toastmasters Web site explains, its goal is to help people become more competent and comfortable in front of an audience. Toastmasters is a nonprofit organization with nearly 250,000 members in more than 12,000 clubs in 106 countries. Most Toastmasters groups are comprised of approximately 20 people who meet weekly for an hour or two. There is no instructor; instead, each speech and meeting is critiqued by a member in a positive manner, focusing on what was done right and what could be improved.

When Myra, whom I work with, came to me in 2003 with the idea of starting a Toastmasters club in our office, I jumped at the idea. I had seen Myra go from being someone who was completely terrified of speaking in public to one of the best public speakers I had ever seen. She told me it was all due to her participation in a Toastmasters club. At the Toastmasters demonstration meeting a bunch of us attended, Dan Karlan, a Toastmasters veteran, told us: "If you came to learn, join us, you may have some fun. If you came to have fun, join us, you may learn something." The experience lived up to his pitch. It was terrific. When we started our club, I was a reasonably accomplished public speaker. In fact, I loved public speaking. I had no idea how much better and how much more confident I could be. I had no clue about timing my speeches, and I didn't realize how often I was saying "um." I hadn't ever memorized a speech before, and I improved in all those areas, thanks to my Toastmasters "coaches" — my fellow participants who provided constructive criticism about my speaking. I also had the opportunity to be an evaluator, and I learned from that as well. Check out Toastmasters. You'll learn a lot.

✳ Grammar

I constantly strive to improve my grammar. It was only as an adult that I learned when to use "I" and when to use "me." It was as an adult that a friend told me I used the word "myself" too often in sales presentations — which helped me to stop overusing that word. I've read grammar books. I've also become a bit of a grammar policeman, correcting other people's grammar — in part because I'm sensitive to my own mistakes, especially with punctuation. And I am not alone. I know employers who refuse to hire anyone who has a typo in his résumé or in a post-interview thank-you note.

If you can learn one grammar rule, learn the difference between plurals and possessives ("there are two dogs" versus "the dog's house" versus "the two dogs' house"). Once you master this, you'll begin to notice how frequently people make errors. For example, you may go into a restaurant and see "try the chefs special" on the menu; it should be "try the chef's special." If you want to read an entertaining grammar book, I recommend the best-seller *Eats, Shoots & Leaves: The Zero Tolerance Approach to Punctuation* by Lynne Truss. It will teach you a lot and also amuse you. Be careful, though, about how far you go in correcting people's bad grammar. In 2008 two anti-typo-vigilantes were sentenced to probation and were banned from national parks for a year after they removed an extraneous apostrophe and added a missing comma to a 60-year-old, hand-painted sign at Grand Canyon National Park.

Most people would benefit from some improvement in their grammar skills (unless all grammar rules are discarded in favor of text messaging's abbreviations, acronyms, and lack of punctuation).

✳ Attending Seminars and Lectures

Since my kids started school, I've attended nearly every lecture offered to parents by our town's schools — programs on self-esteem for teens; drug- and alcohol-abuse prevention; bullying prevention (I wish we had that when I was a kid); safe Internet use for kids; child-assault prevention; college planning; and many other important topics.

I attend lectures at my house of worship and the local community center, and seminars given by our town historical society and various business networking groups. I've attended many industry conferences where I've learned best practices in my profession and have had the opportunity to listen to wonderful keynote speakers. (My dad started a wonderful best practices group for the insurance industry, Intersure, which has been a tremendous asset for our firm's development.)

I also participate in a quarterly discussion group. It's like a book club: All members of the group read the same book each quarter and then come together to discuss it. In addition, we circulate and discuss articles on a wide range of subjects. This is a great way to broaden your horizons; you learn from the articles and from the discussions, and you spend time with terrific, interesting people.

✳ Playing Sports as an Adult

I took a few tennis lessons as a kid, and then over the years I played when the opportunity arose, but that wasn't very often. All of my children were exposed to tennis at a relatively young age, but they didn't play much either at first. Then, in 2007, my daughter Julie decided to take lessons because she wanted to make the high school tennis team (she did). In between the weekly lessons, she and I tried to get out and play once a week, so she could practice what she had learned. I mentioned this to my friend Jeff, who lives about 10 minutes from me. Jeff and I had played some tennis together when we were kids. He suggested that perhaps he and I could go out and hit some time. So we did. And we've played nearly every week since. Jeff gave me some advice, and I got more formal instruction from tennis lessons that my family bought me for my birthday. I also (of course) read some books on tennis. My goal is simply to have fun (which includes trying to win — I do enjoy winning). I've become a much better player, I'm enjoying it, it's good exercise, and it all started after age 44. Pretty cool.

One of my favorite quotes comes from tennis. The quote is from Brad Gilbert, the former professional tennis player who has coached champions Andre Agassi, Andy Roddick, and Andy Murray, and I read it in the book *In the Zone: Achieving Optimal Performance in Business-As in Sports,* by J. Mitchell Perry and Steve Jamison. Discussing the importance of a positive attitude, Gilbert says: "When you beat up on yourself during a match, you've doubled the number of people trying to defeat you." That's a great line to think about in any endeavor.

✳ Learning Foreign Languages

When I was in middle school, I learned French. I enjoyed the experience, and I was able to use my French skills when Marcie and I spent an incredible week in Paris in 1984 during our post-college backpacking trip, and again when I had the good fortune to spend a week there in 1986.

While I never regretted choosing French, I always wished that I knew Spanish because it's so prevalent, especially in the New York area. In early 2006, for reasons I cannot recall, I had two conversations within a very short period of time about the idea of learning Spanish. Very soon after that, I was sitting next to a cousin at a family function and she filled me in on her son's career. She told me that he distributed personal-development products, including foreign language CDs. It seemed like fate. I got the info about his company, learned about the program he sold (PimsleurApproach.com), and ordered the first CD, Spanish I. What appealed to me about the program was that it was strictly listen and repeat. No homework. For 30 days I listened to Spanish and repeated while driving in my car. If I wasn't going to be in the car, I listened on a portable CD player. I gained a basic, rudimentary understanding of Spanish and I loved it. I went from no Spanish to some Spanish in a very short period of time. It felt great. I liked it so much that I bought and completed Spanish II and Spanish III. I don't use my Spanish very often, but it's more than I use my French, and I certainly hear Spanish spoken all the time. While I can't catch a lot of what is being said, I pick up some of it, and that's fun.

✳ Travel

Related to foreign languages is the subject of travel. There is so much to see and learn in this big, wonderful world of ours. Travel is one of the all-time great learning experiences. This, of course, applies to visiting foreign countries, but travel doesn't have to be overseas. There are a limitless number of things to see and learn here in North America. In fact, most of us could spend years' worth of vacations visiting new places and trying new activities within driving distance of where we live. In my case, checking out all that one can experience in the states of New York and New Jersey — and maybe even sightseeing in New York City alone — could fill many vacations. I'm one of those people who doesn't take local sights for granted. I've been to the top of the Empire State Building many times. I've taken the Circle Line boat tour around Manhattan many times. I love going to Broadway shows, visiting museums, and sampling the many other cultural activities that New York City offers — and I recommend that you take advantage of all the opportunities where you live.

❋ Learning From Experiences

In Chapter 4, Be Organized, I talked about not reinventing the wheel. After you do something once, you want to build on the experience by repeating what works and eliminating mistakes. I'm far from perfect, but I try to always learn from my experiences. Comedian Steven Wright jokes that experience is something you don't get until just after you need it. He's right, but only regarding the first time you go through something. Many things happen to us more than one time, so experience is also something you get *before* you need it the *next* time.

Most of the experiences I have shared with you in this book are positive ones — all kinds of experiences and learning that have improved my life by helping me be happier, nicer, more of a leader, and more organized. In this chapter, I share a bunch of the lessons I have learned from mistakes and negative experiences. If something goes well, make the most of that experience by figuring out what you did right and doing it again. And if you have a bad experience, recognize that as an opportunity as well. We can't eliminate negative experiences. We need to accept them, and even embrace them, because they can help us create new and better ways of doing things. As Dan Sullivan and Catherine Nomura of Strategic

Coach® explain in their book, *The Laws of Lifetime Growth*, you don't get to choose all the experiences you have, but you *do* get to choose what to do with those experiences. If we choose to learn from negative experiences, rather than just lamenting them, we make progress and improve our lives. A participant at one Strategic Coach® workshop that I attended made this point beautifully: "If things are stinky, use them as fertilizer."

Mistakes happen. In fact, they're necessary. Growth cannot be achieved without taking risks, but when we take risks, mistakes inevitably will be made. Earlier in the book, for example, we discussed the importance of delegating — as a way to free yourself up to do the things you are great at and love to do, and also as a way to be a good leader. When you delegate, you have to expect that mistakes will occur. The key thing is to always learn from our mistakes. As Dan Sullivan told me, "There are two teams — the winning team and the learning team."

I have often said to people at my company that mistakes are not good, but they are only unacceptable if we repeat them. Not everyone is great about learning from mistakes. So at our office, each time we make a mistake we document it and create a new procedure to avoid the mistake's recurrence. We want to ensure that our company is a "learning organization" — a term I learned early in my career from Peter M. Senge's *The Fifth Discipline: The Art & Practice of the Learning Organization*. A company (or a team or any other group) will be more successful if it is a learning organization. And as an individual, you will be happier and more successful if you are a learning person — a lifelong learner.

✳ How I Learned the Importance of Good Communication

In 1990, when I had been in the insurance business for about three years, I met the managing partner of an accounting firm. We'll call him Mr. Ring. We discussed a program that would give his firm better coverage for a lower cost than he had been paying. I got the information I needed from Mr. Ring and submitted it to the insurance company. Mr. Ring's insurance was not due to renew until months later, but he was willing to move sooner to the better package we were offering, so I followed up weekly with the insurance company. But the insurance company people kept putting off the paperwork for the coverage change because they felt it wasn't urgent. Each week they apologized and told me they would get to it the following week. As the weeks went by, I kept having this conversation with myself: "Maybe I should call Mr. Ring to tell him what's going on...But why should I call him to say I don't have anything yet?...I'll just wait until next week when I have it." Then, the more time that went by, the more I felt that it was pointless to call him unless I could tell him that the change had been finalized. Anyone who knows the right way to do things has already recognized the fallacy in my thinking, and won't be surprised that when I finally called Mr. Ring, he balled me out about how long it had taken and said, "If that's the kind of service you give, I have no interest in working with you, no matter how good your program supposedly is." Ouch!

That experience was so embarrassing that I was never going to let it happen to me again. (It was also financially costly, but the financial pain wasn't as bad as the embarrassment. I felt stupid and incompetent.) Since that time, if I am going to deliver something to someone, I come to an agreement about what the other person expects, and when they expect it. If, for whatever reason, I am going to be unable to deliver what they're expecting, or unable to do so in a timely fashion, I promptly update them and try to agree to a revised plan. This is a wonderful way for all of us to conduct ourselves in every endeavor.

✸ Using the Right Words

Sometimes we have to be told that particular words are inappropriate.

For example, my niece Rebecca (my brother's daughter) is in a school for children with autism. Through my interaction with Rebecca and her family, I learned that the word "retarded," which used to be used fairly commonly, is no longer an acceptable term. A few years ago the Special Olympics, as part of its efforts to eradicate discrimination against people with intellectual disabilities, launched a campaign to eliminate the use of the word "retarded." In early 2009, the organization began its "Spread the Word to End the Word" program (go to r-word.org for more information) and declared March 31, 2009, as the first "Global Day to Eradicate the R-word." Coincidentally, that same month President Obama had to apologize for a comment he made during his appearance on *The Tonight Show With Jay Leno* that seemed insulting to people with disabilities. The president was talking about his lack of bowling skills. When he said that he had been practicing at the White House bowling alley and had recently scored 129, Leno replied, "Oh, no, that's very good." The President then joked, "It was like the Special Olympics or something." I expect a lot more from the President of the United States. I am sure that the President is a lifelong learner, and that he quickly learned from that experience.

✳ Learning About the Words "Boys" and "Girls"

Like the president, I learned the hard way about using the right words. One day when I was in high school, my friend and I were sitting alone in a classroom. It was lunch period and we had arrived a bit early to our next class. As we sat there talking, two more students walked in. One of them said to his friend, referring to us, "Look at the faggots we have in our class. They get here so early." (Now, before we go on, I want to point out that their comment was pretty typical bullying in my high school. It could have been said to us by a kid with white skin or a kid with black skin. In this case, it happened to have been said by a black student, which becomes important in a moment.)

In response, I said, "You boys are here pretty early too," at which point he threw me against the wall and choked me for a few scary seconds, telling me to never use the word "boy" again. I had no clue about the racially charged history of the word "boy," that it had long been used in a racist, disrespectful way toward black men. (I probably would have known if I had been more of a reader at that age.) It was normal for me to refer to all males my age as boys — in fact, I still refer to my closest groups of high school and college friends as "The Boys," and when I enter a room full of my buddies, it's fairly typical for me to say, "What's up boys?" I had friends of all backgrounds as I grew up in Teaneck, New Jersey, but no one ever told me about the "boy" thing. Only later did I figure out what I had done wrong — why he had reacted the way he did. I'm generally a quick learner. Getting choked undoubtedly accelerated my learning.

In early 2009, an incident in an NBA game reminded me of that high school experience. A referee named Derrick Stafford ruled that Vince Carter (then with the New Jersey Nets, and at one time one of my favorite players) had knocked a ball out of bounds. When Carter disputed the call, he was assessed a technical foul, which gives a free foul shot to the other team. Carter screamed at the ref, who assessed a second technical foul, which meant that Carter was ejected from the game. Carter had to be restrained and he was escorted off the court. Before that incident, Carter had been ejected from a game only once before in his time with the Nets. It was subsequently reported that Carter had become incensed because the referee had called him "boy." The league acknowledged that Stafford — who, like Carter, is African-American — had used the charged term but did not discipline either the player or the referee.

After learning in high school about the words "boys" and "men," in college I learned about the words "girls" and "women."

My big activity during college was my involvement with the school radio station. I joined the station as a freshman, became an on-air disc jockey, and worked my way up until I was elected the station's general manger during my senior year. Soon after the election, I was sitting in the cafeteria with my friends Teri and Gail.

I don't recall exactly what I said, but somewhere in our conversation I used the word "girl." It could have been something like, "I'm going up for a drink refill. Do either of you girls want anything?" They looked at each other, looked at me, and then one of them said, "David, sit down, we want to talk with you about something." I sat, and one of them continued, "Don't take this personally, but now that you're going to be GM of the radio station, you can't say 'girls' anymore."

I didn't have the faintest idea what she was talking about and I said so.

They explained: "Females our age are not girls. We're women. You're going to run a major campus organization. You're going to want people to look to you for leadership. You have to set an example. We're women now, not girls. You need to call us women or you won't get the respect you want, the respect you deserve, and the respect you'll need."

Until that time, the only people I thought of as women were my mother, my aunts, and my teachers. My friends were not women. They were girls. Just like my male friends were boys. I told this to Teri and Gail. They explained that this was different: "Males get to be called 'guys,' but you never hear anyone calling us 'gals,' right? It's got to be 'men and women,' or 'guys and women' if you want to do that, or even 'boys and women' — but not 'girls' anymore. Trust us."

I *did* trust them. They had no reason to steer me wrong. They were two of my closest friends. So I started to refer to females as women. It felt odd. It felt uncomfortable. But I stuck with it. After about 21 days (the length of time it takes to form a new habit), I realized that it no longer felt uncomfortable. In fact, the opposite became the case: It felt uncomfortable to hear females referred to as girls. My friends had done a major favor for me, and I carried the lesson into my life as a grown-up.

Several years later I began working with my dad and I taught him about referring to females as "women." My dad was born in 1935. He's been a successful business person. While he was never sexist, he referred to all secretaries as "girls." I heard him say things such as, "Have your girl call my girl" and "I'll have my girl send it to you." I needed to help him adopt the modern terminology. And he did it — displaying his aptitude for lifelong learning.

✳ A Nose That Got Broken, Back in Hoboken

The title of this section is a line from a song my friend Benny wrote, in part commemorating my most painful (physically) and dangerous learning experience.

Late one night in 1987, I was eating at a diner in Hoboken, New Jersey, with a bunch of my closest friends. I was sitting across from Benny, who was facing the restaurant. When the waitress came over to take our order, Benny said to her, while pointing someone out, "That guy over there, he stole your tip from that other table." She looked and said, "Oh, that guy," in a way that suggested she recognized him and wasn't surprised by his criminal behavior.

A few minutes later, the guy, who was huge, was standing right next to me and looking down menacingly at Benny. "Which one of you tough guys is gonna say I stole the tip?" he asked.

Benny said, "None of us. We don't want any trouble."

The guy kept repeating the question, each time getting closer and closer to Benny. Just before Benny was about to be attacked, I jumped up — and promptly got decked. I remember seeing a giant fist come flying toward my nose. I remember the guy jumping on me and punching my back as I was doubled over, looking down at a pool of blood. The "fight," if you can call it that, was quickly broken up.

My friends sat me down. There was a giant mirror on the wall behind me and I turned to look at myself, but my friend Mark told me not to. I did anyway, and my nose looked like the letter S. I could see why Mark didn't want me to look. That freaked me out a bit.

Meanwhile, the guy who attacked me stuck around long enough for the cops to come and arrest him.

I went to the emergency room at St. Mary's Hospital, got an X-ray, and was told that my nose was broken, though I had already figured that out.

The next day I went to an ear, nose and throat specialist (ENT). The ENT gave me a shot — the needle looked awfully big as it headed into my nostril — and then as he was feeling my nose, saying, "Yes, I think what we need to do is…" I heard and felt something cracking as he broke my nose again. He then explained that he had to break it to set it properly, and that he wanted to surprise me so that I wouldn't tense up.

After my nose was set, I went to the police station and filed a complaint against my attacker. I was shown a card with six photos on it. I instantly picked out the guy and the officer said, "Oh, yeah, him," as in "Sure, we know him, he's a regular here."

A week later, in the Hoboken newspaper, I looked to see whether I had made the police blotter, which was usually pretty humorous, and, sure enough, true to form, the headline read, "Man Breaks Nose on Fist."

About a year later, I had to have surgery to correct a breathing problem I had developed because I had a deviated septum from the punch. (They had to break my nose again for the surgery, so that's three broken noses in all.) A week after the surgery, my nose started bleeding. And it wouldn't stop. I got a towel, ran outside of my New York City apartment building, and hailed a cab. (In hindsight, I should have called an ambulance, but I didn't even think of that. My only thought was whether I should drive myself, which I had quickly ruled out.)

At the hospital, they worked on me for hours until they finally stopped the bleeding. A few hours later, while I was still resting at the hospital, it started again. As they worked on me the second time, they said that if it didn't stop soon I would need surgery and a blood transfusion. It stopped, and then a couple of hours later it started one more time.

They finally stopped it for good by shoving a cotton pad — or some such thing — down my throat, with strings on it that they pulled up through my nose. I was afraid that if I sneezed, or even swallowed too hard, I would start bleeding again. I was in the hospital a few more days recuperating and then went home, gaunt and pale. I ate liver every night for about a month to get the iron needed to build up my blood count.

I never imagined that the broken nose incident would lead to a dangerous medical problem. But it could have been even worse. A punch to the nose can be deadly. And as Marcie (then my fiancé, now my wife) said to me at the time, "What if that guy had a gun?"

I learned a significant lesson. I can't say I've never had a confrontation with another person since that night in the diner (you've already read about some of the wrongheaded things I've done since that time), but that experience certainly helped me avoid many situations that might have turned ugly. Road rage is one example. It wasn't too long after my nose incident that numerous violent and deadly road rage events appeared in the news. I learned that it wouldn't be a smart idea to have a confrontation with anyone on the road — even something as small as a dirty look can provoke a violent reaction. I've learned to recognize the warning signs of my rage, and when I feel that rush of anger I tell myself to calm down and walk away instead of letting my temper get the best of me.

✳ My Father and the Racist

As a person of Jewish descent in the New York area, I have few recollections of finding myself the victim of racism. That made it all the more incredible to me when I was a teen and I met a blatant racist during a family vacation at a dude ranch in Arizona (where we rode horses, ate at outdoor barbeques and campfires, and had an all-around great time). One day, after the morning ride, my dad and I were sitting with one of the ranch hands, a gentleman who had been working at the ranch for a long time. I don't know how old he was, but he seemed to be older than my dad, who was in his early forties at the time. As we talked, the rancher said something we found stunning. So far, as of age 5, his son hadn't been off the ranch yet. Something more stunning came next when he said, "But someday he'll have to meet the niggers and the kikes." My eyes widened as I looked at my dad. My dad looked at me, shook his head, and told the rancher we had to get going. As we walked off, my dad explained to me that the rancher wasn't the last ignorant person I would ever meet.

My dad could have gotten angry, he could have admonished the rancher, yelled at him, or even gotten into a fistfight. Instead, he walked away. And I know that my dad's way was the better way, that fighting is not the best solution. It's better to walk away feeling pity for how ignorant the other person is. (One can debate whether it's better to at least say something in that kind of situation, and what would be best to say, but fighting is still not the answer.) Thomas Jefferson explained the better way when he said, "Nothing gives one person so much advantage over another as to remain always cool and unruffled under all circumstances." Easier said than done — and very much worth aspiring to.

✳ Desperate = Dumb; Learning About Getting Ripped Off

The day that I started my first job out of college, in the fall of 1984, I began to search for an apartment in New York City. I was living with my parents, in my childhood bedroom in Teaneck, New Jersey, and though I was close to New York City, I was eager to move to Manhattan, which would result in a far shorter commute, plus a far more enjoyable social life.

As is generally the case in Manhattan, finding an affordable apartment proved to be extremely difficult and frustrating. The search lasted for months, and then on February 18, 1985, I read this ad in the *New York Times*:

> GREENWICH VILLAGE NR 7TH AVE
> Partially furnished apt, walk up,
> excellent location. $750.

I had heard the "rule" about not spending more than 25 percent of my salary on housing. I had thrown that rule out the window months earlier. The $750 rent was about 43 percent of my salary.

I called the phone number in the ad and spoke with a guy named Steve Feldman. He told me that he was moving into his girlfriend's apartment and needed to sublet this one. He also told me that the amount in the ad was incorrect, that the rent was only $500!

During my lunch hour, I met him at the apartment. It was a great location, but the apartment was on the sixth floor, meaning I would have to walk up five flights of stairs. And it was tiny and dirty. I jumped at it.

Feldman said he would put together a lease and would require $1,000, "the normal first month's rent and one month's security deposit." He insisted on cash and asked me for $100 on the spot to hold the apartment until we could get together again the next day to sign the lease. I gave him the $100 and had him sign a receipt I wrote out.

Giving him $900 in cash the next day didn't seem like the greatest idea, but this was the dog-eat-dog world of Manhattan apartment-hunting, which seemed to have its own rules about everything. Many people in similar situations would not have done it. But an even greater number probably would have felt as desperate as I did, and would have handed over the cash.

I was set to move in on March 15. Then, when the day arrived and it was time to get my key, Steve Feldman had disappeared.

I called and called and called and couldn't get through to him.

He never answered the phone. Then the number was disconnected.

I went to the apartment — *my* apartment. Someone else was living in it — someone who had *also* sublet it from Steve Feldman. He told me that I was one of a bunch of people who had shown up over the previous several days looking for Feldman, having sublet the apartment from him. I went to the police and they told me that Feldman had ripped off over a dozen people, making off with more than $17,000.

I was not a happy camper, to say the least. Not only didn't I have a Manhattan apartment, but I had been robbed of $1,000!

The police found Steve Feldman a few weeks later. He had $4,500 in cash on him, which the police seized and divided up proportionately among the victims. I got back about $250. We were supposed to get full restitution eventually. I never saw another penny. I learned a lesson about the mistakes you can make when you're desperate. I also learned something that has been said by many people, many times, in many situations — if a deal looks too good to be true, it probably is. Steve Feldman taught me a lesson worth far more than the $750 he stole from me.

✳ Scalped

When my son Jeremy was 13, he and I, his best friend Sam, and Sam's dad, Bob, went to see the Allman Brothers at the Beacon Theater in Manhattan. I thought it was great that Jeremy and Sam were Allman Brothers fans, because I was a longtime fan. I hadn't been to an Allmans concert since I was a teen, and Jeremy and Sam had never been to a rock concert.

The shows sold out quickly and Bob bought tickets for us, his treat, from a ticket broker. The following year, the boys said they wanted to go again, and it sounded like the beginning of a great tradition. Again, we weren't quick enough to buy tickets before the shows sold out. That's when Bob revealed to me that he had paid a huge sum for the tickets the previous year. He said he didn't want to do that again, and I completely agreed. We decided we would go to the theater on the night of a concert and try to buy tickets out front.

Bob called me on the morning of the show and told me that he had gone with a friend to the Allmans the night before. They had bought tickets out front — $85 tickets for $150 each — and the show was awesome. That evening, we took the boys for pizza and then started walking to the Beacon. About a block and a half from the theater, we encountered the first ticket seller. He wanted $150 per ticket and said he had second-row seats. It seemed too good to be true — which should have been a clue that something was wrong. Unfortunately, I hadn't sufficiently learned my "if it seems too good to be true, it probably is" lesson during the apartment scandal of 20 years earlier. After Bob bargained the ticket scalper down to $120 per seat, we made the purchase.

Sadly, when we got to the theater we learned that the tickets were fakes, and a security guard at the door confiscated them.

The kids' immediate reaction was disappointment about the money that was lost. "That's so much money, $240 for each family," one of them said. We agreed that it was a lot of money, but I explained that it was actually a relatively small amount in the larger scheme of things (a lesson about not sweating the small stuff) and that it was a small price to pay for a big lesson about the possibility of getting ripped off by unscrupulous people — a lesson that hopefully would help Jeremy and Sam avoid such dangers in the future. We took the boys for ice cream and had a lot of laughs. We joked about how stupid it had been to buy those tickets.

When we got home, Marcie and my daughters were surprised to see us so early. One of my daughters was horrified by the lost dollars and I explained that it wasn't about the money. We would have spent the same amount if the tickets had been real — probably a bit more, in fact. But instead of seeing the Allmans, we had lots of laughs, a bit of learning, and definitely an unforgettable night.

✳ A Few Important Things I Learned From My Parents

My father taught me the importance of being persistent. My dad *never* gives up. It's an extremely valuable trait. My brother, too, is very persistent. He was that way as a child, and he is that way today, and his persistence is a big reason why he is extremely successful at whatever he sets out to accomplish. .

My father also taught me about resilience. If you're a salesperson, you're not going to be successful every time you try to make a sale. You need to be able to bounce back from each defeat and move forward. Confucius said, "Our greatest glory is not in never falling, but in rising every time we fall."

Both my father and I are good at putting things behind us. Sometimes he and I have heated discussions, but only moments later it's like it never happened. We move on. I give my father a lot of credit for that, and consider that to be one of the secrets of our success.

My father also taught me that when you passionately believe in something, you don't have to be afraid of standing up for your idea of sharing it with others — in fact, you're performing a public service by doing so. As a salesperson, this is very important. The only way you can be successful at selling is to believe in what you are selling. If you believe in your product or service, then you know that you're helping others by educating them about it and giving them the opportunity to decide whether they want to buy it.

I thank my mother for teaching me the importance of a healthy lifestyle. I learned many of my good eating habits from my mom, and I learned from her to be an advocate for my own health by continuously reading to stay up on the latest health trends.

I also learned from my parents to be optimistic, something I have tried very hard to pass along to my children. Optimism doesn't guarantee that things will work out well, but you're more likely to succeed if you're optimistic than if you're pessimistic — and, just as important, you'll spend a lot less time and energy worrying. In addition to optimism about the future, my parents taught me to look at the bright side of things that have already happened. After Steve Feldman ripped me off, my mom said to me, "Well, you learned a lesson. And you can be happy you didn't lose $1,500."

(When Feldman inexplicably reduced the rent from $750 to $500 — probably to increase the chances that I wouldn't back out — he also reduced the required security deposit from $1,500 to $1,000.) While it was hard to be happy about any part of the scam, when my parents said I could "be happy," I didn't argue with them and I wasn't surprised. I'd been hearing that all my life. For example, if they heard about a car accident, and none of the passengers had been injured, my parents would always say, "At least no one got hurt." The car might have been totaled, but my parents were talking about how "lucky" the passengers were. When a grandparent or a great-aunt or great-uncle passed away, it was always, "At least he/she didn't suffer." On a more mundane matter, if my dad and I went to a Mets game and watched the Mets lose a close one, he would say on the car ride home, "Well, at least it was a close game."

Apparently that stuff sinks in. During the NBA play-offs one year, I was with my friend Alex the day after a Nets loss. "Too bad the Nets got blown out last night," he said. I responded, "On the bright side, it was clear pretty early that it was over, so I got to bed early." Then he said to me, "One thing I always love about you — and I hope you never lose that — you always see the positive in everything." I know we're talking about sports here, not life and death, but Alex was right about my positive take on things. I love sports and I follow my favorite teams pretty closely. Because those teams rarely win a championship, there is quite a bit of disappointment every year — which is the case for most sports fans. But because tickets to professional play-off games are so expensive, and the games start so late at night, I help myself get over the end of my team's season by noting that I won't have to spend any more money on tickets and I'll be able to get to bed earlier in the ensuing days.

In addition, many of the things that go wrong for us end up working out for the best. Two of my closest friends were a longtime couple when we were in college and for a bunch of years after. They seemed destined to marry and live happily ever after. When they broke up, it was a big deal. Today, they are each married, with beautiful, wonderful kids — and they wouldn't have it any other way. It's not like the movies, which are filled with marriages in which one of the spouses regrets "the one that got away." In real life, because we know that no marriage is perfect, the one we are in is perfect for us. And if you have kids, there is no way you can regret the one that got away, because the one you ended up with brought you to the place you are at now, with the kids you wouldn't trade for anything. On a similar note, my buddy Steve became a first-time dad (to twins) at age 46. Did he wish he could have been a dad sooner? Yes. Does he regret not having kids sooner? No way. If he did, he wouldn't have these two kids he loves more than anything.

After the apartment scam that I described earlier, I found a better apartment, with the help of networking. I was telling everyone my sad story, and many of the people that I told were then sharing the story with others. Marcie's cousin heard the story and told me about an apartment in his building that was going to be available as a sublet for $500 a month. It was also in the West Village, relatively near the "Steve Feldman" apartment, but the building was much nicer, the apartment was larger, and it was on the second floor instead of the sixth. Everything worked out even better than it would have had the Steve Feldman apartment been real. In fact, it worked out *because* of the scam experience. If I hadn't been telling everyone my tale of woe, I wouldn't have found the great apartment.

Ronald Reagan reported in his autobiography, *An American Life*, that his mother was a big advocate of the idea that everything works out for the best. Reagan wrote that his mother taught him that if things go wrong, you have to move on and not get down. She explained that later on he would be able to see that some good thing in his life would not have happened if certain bad experiences hadn't happened first, which is often referred to as, "when one door closes, another one opens."

My friend Josh tells a great story. He once had a terrible bout with food poisoning. When he had almost completely recuperated, he went on a date. The date went fine, but the brief relationship that ensued had an annoying by-product: He caught mononucleosis from her, possibly due, in part, to his body's weakened condition after the food poisoning. A year later, while dating someone else, Josh had a (rare) relapse of the mono. As usually seems to happen only in movies, his new girlfriend nursed him back to health, they fell in love, and now they're married with a child. Without the food poisoning, none of this would have happened.

Ringo Starr had a similar story. In *The Beatles: The Biography,* author Bob Spitz explains that while Ringo was suffering through a long, difficult hospitalization, he was introduced to the drums. That worked out pretty well.

✳ "You'll Understand When You're a Grown-Up"…Maybe

As I've said, you don't have to reinvent the wheel. But you can adapt what you learn in ways that work for you. My approach to parenting is a good example. As I've said, I learned many good things from my parents, and they influenced many of the choices that I made as a parent. I now understand some of the concerns they had that led to the strict rules they imposed when I was growing up. But my parents had some rules that seemed ridiculous to me then and that I still don't agree with — so those rules I did *not* adopt when it was my turn to be a parent.

When I was a kid I had to keep my hair short. This was in the late 1960s (think Woodstock) and early 1970s — short hair was definitely not in, except in our house. And my parents had a pretty strict dress code for us. They felt it would reflect poorly on them if I wore T-shirts or torn jeans to school (or if I had long hair). My parents also didn't allow us to sleep over at other kids' houses. They said, "We don't know what things those people do at their houses" (I imagined devil worship and sexual deviancy). They made an exception only for friends whom I would visit for the weekend because they lived a bit of a drive from our town.

On the hairstyle and dress-code issues, I took my cue from my mother-in-law. Marcie has older siblings, including Stewart, who is eight years older — which means that he attended high school during the heart of the Woodstock era. Early in my relationship with Marcie, we were looking through some photo albums at her house and I saw a picture of Stewart when he was in high school, looking very hippie-like. At this point I had known my future mother-in-law for only a short while and I thought of her as a conservative person. I figured she would have had the same kinds of rules as my parents had, and I talked to her about the picture. "I'm surprised you let Stew dress like that," I said. "And that long hair." She responded: "I didn't care how they dressed. I didn't care how they wore their hair. All I cared about was that they were good kids." Nice. That's the approach I embraced.

As to sleepovers, Marcie and I let our kids stay at friends' houses after we had met the parents and gotten a look inside the house — which didn't do a lot, but at least it took away the unknown and gave us some sort of comfort level. We also spoke to our kids about potential dangers, such as improper physical contact (and other things we learned about from *Protecting the Gift*, one of the parenting books I mentioned earlier in this chapter). And our kids slept out, or had their friends sleep over, virtually every weekend for a span of about eight years during elementary school and middle school.

Sleepovers can be great experiences for kids because they're able to observe and learn from other families. In my case, the learning came from one of the places I was allowed to sleep out at — my friend Bobby's house. Bobby and I met at summer camp. He lived a few towns away and we didn't go to school together, so we didn't get together often — and when we did, it usually involved a sleepover. The first time I slept at his house, after we ate breakfast, we got dressed and got ready to go out for the day. Before we left, his mother, a wonderful woman named Barbara, taught me about proper sleepover etiquette. "You didn't make your bed," she said to me. "When you sleep at someone's house, you don't leave the bed unmade. Please take the sheets off the bed, fold the blankets, and fold the bed back up into the couch." I did as she asked — and went on to do that without being asked every subsequent time I slept at their house, and every time I have been anyone's houseguest since then. How do you learn how to be a proper grown-up houseguest? You learn by being a houseguest when you're a kid.

✳ Learner for Life

When I met Jim Atkins, he was 65. He was in the middle of his second career, working as an insurance company executive after selling a business he had founded. In 1994, Jim's work at the company shifted to a 50 percent schedule and Jim began to advise my firm as a consultant, which took up most of the other 50 percent of his time. Jim helped us grow our business, and I learned a ton from him. Perhaps Jim's greatest gift to me, and everyone else he has touched, is the example he has set of lifelong learning. It was fascinating watching Jim continue to learn and grow. He was always reading, attending seminars, and picking up knowledge from his wide-ranging experiences. Lifelong learning has been part of Jim's secret to staying young — along with his daily exercise regimen and watching what he eats. While he was still working with us, and after he ceased working with the insurance company, Jim, then in his seventies, helped his wife with her fledgling business, a dance school and dance company. It was yet another learning experience for Jim, and he embraced it with the same vigor with which he approached every other experience in his very full and fulfilling life. More recently, Jim told me that he and one of his younger friends — a gentleman I know who is in his seventies — were taking college classes together, just for the fun of learning.

Jim, now in his mid-eighties and going strong, is one of many great models for all of us to emulate. The actress and singer Eartha Kitt, who passed away in 2008, was another lifelong learner. She once said, "I am learning all the time. The tombstone will be my diploma." That's a great commitment to lifelong learning! Abe Lincoln emphasized the importance of lifelong learning when he said, "I don't think much of a man who is not wiser today than he was yesterday."

Learning is interesting. Learning is good for your mental health — and your mental health is good for your physical health. The world will keep changing and if we don't keep learning, we'll be left behind. As we discussed at the beginning of this chapter, Abraham Maslow said that humans have an instinctual need to make the most of their abilities and to strive to be the best they can be. Learning helps us reach our full potential. If you've stopped learning, I hope this chapter has helped you find some of the myriad things you can learn — everything from facts to foreign languages to how to avoid repeating mistakes — and has shown you ways to learn, such as by reading, traveling, or through other experiences.

Think of all the people who grew up long before computers were everywhere and now communicate with their grandchildren via Facebook, Skype, and texting. You *can* teach an old dog new tricks. It's never too late to learn. And with the Internet, learning is easier than ever. Ask yourself regularly, "Am I being a lifelong learner?" If the answer is yes, keep it up. If the answer is no, the time to start learning is now.

✳ New Habits and Progress

Remember: *Life is long*, meaning we have time. If we try to make a million changes all at once, we often end up so overwhelmed that we make none. Instead, if we *slow down to make the changes*, and then *stop to celebrate the progress*, we'll accomplish much more.

Slow Down to Make the Changes — It takes 21 days to form a new habit. What are some ideas you have for new habits you would like to adopt following your reading of Chapter 5?

Stop to Celebrate the Progress — Remember to look back on all that you've accomplished. What are some areas of progress you've made?

Chapter 6

Be Healthy

"I intend to live forever...so far, so good." — Steven Wright

Now is a great time in history to be alive. People are living longer than ever. Science helps us learn about the secrets to long life (foods, living habits, vitamins — it's like there really is a fountain of youth) and helps people survive diseases that in the past were a death sentence. My father's sister died of cancer in the 1960s, when she was only in her thirties. My dad's mom died of cancer in the 1970s, in her sixties. But his other sister is a cancer survivor — she won a battle with cancer in the 1990s, in *her* sixties. My college buddy is a cancer survivor. The moms of at least two of my daughters' friends are cancer survivors. I know people who are living active lives after triple, quadruple, or quintuple bypass surgery. We just have to do our part to avoid a premature death — eat well, exercise, and minimize unhealthy habits such as smoking and unsafe driving. We can live forever — or at least for a very, very long time.

✳ Living Forever

In their 2009 book, *Transcend: Nine Steps to Living Well Forever*, Ray

Kurzweil and Terry Grossman write about the amazing biotech and nanotech advances that are coming and say their goal is to help readers live long enough to take advantage of those advances. I love that. I've been talking for years about living forever, and now there are books telling us about the importance of living long enough to live forever! Now, before you put down this book because you think I'm crazy, think about this: Even if living forever is a stretch, we are definitely experiencing an extension of our life span and an extension of the number of years we can live in good health — our health span.

The first seeds of my optimism about living forever (or at least a really long time) were planted in my thirties, when I observed that my parents, then in their sixties, seemed so much younger than my grandparents had seemed at the same age. I'm aware that part of that came from a change in my perspective: at one time, 20 seemed old to me, until I got close to 20 myself; then 30 seemed old to me, then 40, then 50. When my grandparents were 70, I was looking at them from the eyes of a child, whereas when I look at my parents at 70, it's from the eyes of a grown-up. Still, when I was a kid, my 70-year-old grandparents were old people. They moved slowly, only one of them got any significant exercise (the one who lived the longest liked to walk), and they looked old. At 70, they looked the way many 90-year-olds look today. While my parents are officially "senior citizens," they are not frail, elderly people. Exercise, better eating habits, and regular medical checkups have helped my parents age more slowly than their parents. In addition, my parents' generation (and all of us) have benefitted from advances in medical technology that were not available to their parents. Today we look around and see so many cancer survivors, such as my father's sister, living vibrant, healthy lives. We see television commercials for cancer centers that help people overcome the disease. When I was a kid — when cancer took my other aunt's life and my grandmother's life — people didn't even talk about the disease, or they referred to it as "the C word."

My parents are not unusual. I see many people in their seventies who look like what 50-year-olds used to look like. I see people over 80, like my mother-in-law, looking like what 60-year-olds used to look like. It's not an exaggeration to say that 80 is the new 60, or 70 is the new 50. It's a reality.

Seeing the jump that my parents made over my grandparents, I decided that I would make the same jump over my parents. I figured that by the time I reached what we call "old age," I would be a bionic man, like Steve Austin in *The Six Million Dollar Man*, the 1970s TV show. As I thought about that future, I would hear excerpts from the show's introduction in my head…"We can rebuild him. We have the technology. We have the capability to build the world's first bionic man…Better, stronger, faster."

Thirty-plus years later, books are being written about advances in technologies like bionics. To live "forever," we may have to have wires and other features that have not traditionally been associated with being human. That's okay with me. And even if that doesn't become reality — even if we can't live forever — why not try to get there? The worst that can happen is that we live longer and healthier lives.

✳ The Fantastic Voyage Through My Body

I had one experience with some pretty awesome medical technology. In late 2007, blood tests from my annual physical showed a low level of a protein called ferritin, which indicated an iron deficiency and caused some concern. My doctor prescribed iron pills and a battery of tests to determine why my level was low (perhaps internal bleeding of some sort). I went through several procedures — an endoscopy, where they looked at my insides through a tiny camera at the end of a tube that was inserted down through my mouth; a colonoscopy; and a CT scan — which showed no abnormalities. But there was a part of my intestines that could not be looked at by those tests. So, for my last test, I had a capsule endoscopy.

The doctor explained: "We're going to give you a pill to swallow. It has a camera in it. With it, we'll be able to take photos of the inside of your small intestine."

He showed me a sample of the camera pill. It was larger than the largest pill I had ever swallowed, but that didn't bother me. What I wondered about was the process. So I asked.

"So I have to look in the toilet and fish this thing out after it passes through me and bring it back here to have you look at it?"

The doctor explained that I wouldn't have to do that. Instead, the camera would transmit photos to a small device that I would wear on my waist all day (it was like wearing a pager). All I had to do was to return the device at the end of the day. The photographs would be downloaded to a computer, and the doctor would review them. Eventually, I would pass the capsule, which I might or might not see before flushing it away.

The procedure went smoothly (and the results were good). When I brought in the device, the technicians let me see a few pictures as they downloaded them. It was so cool. I felt like I was part of the movie *Fantastic Voyage*, in which a microscopic submarine and crew travel through a character's body.

The doctor called me the next day to tell me he saw something that would account for the low levels of ferritin, but that the problem was receding. (The iron pills got my levels back up where they needed to be, and after I stopped taking the iron my levels stayed normal.)

In March 2009, Oprah Winfrey had a show about medical advances, some that had been achieved and others that were predicted for the future. This stuff is so cool — and even more fantastic than my "fantastic voyage." She featured Dr. Anthony Atala, director of the Wake Forest Institute for Regenerative Medicine — as in regenerating body parts. This is not science fiction, this is science fact. Researchers have grown muscles, bones, a working heart valve, and much more. The show then featured a gentleman who had accidentally cut off part of the middle finger on his right hand. His brother happened to be a pioneer in cellular regeneration. Using a powder made from material found in pig bladders, doctors were able to get the finger to grow back!

✳ The Keys to Staying Healthy

We all want to live a long life and feel good along the way. We know that there are a few basic guidelines for achieving that goal. Eating well and exercising are two of the keys. When I say eating well, I'm not talking about dieting. I'm talking about maintaining a balanced diet, avoiding unhealthy foods, and eating fruits, vegetables, and whole grains.

Just because we know which foods are bad for us doesn't mean we're avoiding them. And just because we understand that exercise is important doesn't mean we're doing it. I've always known that many people don't eat well and don't exercise regularly — but I did think things were getting better. I was wrong. The percent of those eating well and exercising has gone down! A study published in the June 2009 issue of *The American Journal of Medicine* compared results from two National Health and Nutrition Examination surveys — one from 2001-2006 and one 1988-1994. The number of Americans ages 40 to 74 who ate five fruits and vegetables a day dropped from 42 percent to 26 percent, while the obesity rate increased from 28 percent to 36 percent. And the percentage of Americans who said they worked out for at least 30 minutes three times a week dropped from more than 50 percent to 43 percent.

Unfortunately, it's extremely hard for many people to change their eating and other lifestyle habits. When people have heart attacks or other serious health problems and are told by their doctors that they will die if they don't eat better and exercise more, they usually *do* change their habits. It's a pity that for many people it takes such a dire situation to make changes. You don't want to play Russian roulette with your life, hoping that you'll be lucky enough not to die before you get that wake-up call. The stakes are very high. If there's a chance that we can live forever, or at least a really long time, we're giving up a lot by behaving in ways that we know can cause premature death.

I have a long-time friend who is one of the lucky ones. Sadly, his dad passed away in his fifties of heart disease when we were in college. Yet, as I adopted healthier eating habits and became an exerciser, he didn't live a particularly healthy lifestyle. Then he had heart bypass surgery in his early forties — which doesn't sound very lucky. But the luck was that this happened to him in an era when people routinely survive that kind of a procedure. Soon after the surgery he told me, "Now I see why you've been eating fish all these years instead of red meat."

My father-in-law also passed away from heart disease when my wife and I were in college — before I got a chance to meet him. He was only 61. Thankfully, Marcie appears to have inherited her mother's health. But she did get one sort of wake-up call. I clipped an article for her from *Prevention* magazine that was titled, "I Refused to Inherit Heart Disease." It was about a 44-year-old woman (Marcie's exact age at the time) with a family history of heart disease who improved her health profile (weight, cholesterol, and blood pressure) through better eating and exercise. Of all the magazine and newspaper articles I passed along to her, that one stayed on her desk for more than two years.

Don't put off adopting a healthier lifestyle. Make it a priority. But, as I've stressed throughout this book, don't try to change everything at once. I've divided this chapter into three parts: eating well; exercising; and other general wellness habits. In each section, you'll see how you can make significant progress with small, manageable improvements.

Be Healthy, Part 1: Eat Well

A lot of people want to lose weight. If that weren't the case, there wouldn't be dozens and dozens of weight-loss programs — from A (Atkins) to Z (Zone), with everything in between. Really. Check it out: Atkins Diet, Biggest Loser Diet, Cookie Diet, Dr. Phil's Ultimate Weight Solution, Eat Right for Your Type, Flat Belly Diet, Grapefruit Diet, Hallelujah Diet, "I" Diet, Jenny Craig, Karl Lagerfeld Diet, LA Weight Loss, Martha's Vineyard Diet Detox, NutriSystem Diet, Ornish Diet, Perricone Diet, Quantum Eating, Rice Diet Solution, South Beach Diet, Thin for Life, UltraMetabolism Diet, Volumetrics, Weight Watchers, X Factor Diet, You — On a Diet, the Zone.

There is so much advice out there about healthy eating habits that it can be overwhelming. I'm going to suggest that you adopt healthful eating the way I did it: slowly. My strategy is not a fad diet. It's not even a diet, per se. I don't like the idea of people going on a diet. I like the idea of people changing their eating habits. Many diets tout quickie solutions that, like the New Year's resolutions I talked about in this book's introduction, are famously short-lived. (If you didn't read the introduction, please go back and read it now, as what we're about to discuss builds directly on material there.) A *Wall Street Journal* article about New Year's resolutions quoted several people whose feelings are similar to mine. Martha Stewart said she believed in constant evolution and change, rather than in New Year's resolutions. And architect Steven Holl said that instead of New Year's resolutions, he made monthly experiments. Both of these approaches are very close to my plan for you. Here we go.

Because it takes 21 days to form a new habit, as we discussed in the introduction, you can form 52 new habits in three years. That's pretty awesome. You take one small step at a time, and after three years you've made 52 changes to your life. Fifty-two changes! That's a lot.

I've identified a kind of "healthy eating's greatest hits" for you: 52 changes for you to make to your eating habits, one at a time, over the next three years. They are not listed in any order. You can choose the order. You can also add to the list.

Remember, *life is long* — you don't have to make a million changes all at once. You don't have to get so overwhelmed about all the changes you have to make that you make none. Instead, plan to make the changes over a long period. Time flies, and the next thing you know, three years will have gone by and you'll have made 52 changes.

I'm not a doctor, so I'm not going to list all the reasons why you should do each of these things. Also, new health recommendations are constantly announced. Later on I'll give you some resources to keep up with the changes that will keep coming.

❋ The 52 Healthy Eating Habits

1. **Eat walnuts** — I've read many articles about the benefits of eating nuts. While the articles vary in their recommendations about particular types of nuts, walnuts are always at or near the top of the list. They are rich in omega-3 fatty acids, which help prevent high cholesterol,

high blood pressure, heart disease, cancer, and many other diseases and conditions. I don't like the taste of walnuts on their own, but I love how they taste when I toss them into my cereal bowl every morning — and my breakfast sustains me longer in the morning now that I've added the protein from the walnuts. Walnuts, like many types of nuts, are also a great snack. I enjoy them mixed with raisins, dried cranberries, or dried blueberries (or fresh blueberries). Many nuts help raise your good cholesterol. In addition to walnuts, I eat almonds, pistachios, peanuts, and pecans. (I love Trader Joe's Sweet & Spicy Pecans. I eat them plain or I throw them into a salad — delicious!)

2. **Eat blueberries** — I also toss blueberries into my cereal bowl every morning. I prefer them fresh, but because it can be a challenge to always have a supply of fresh ones on hand, I also buy dried blueberries (with no sulfites). Frozen blueberries are another good alternative. A huge number of articles in recent years have touted the benefits of blueberries, which are big providers of antioxidants, great sources of fiber, and rich in resveratrol, the anticancer and heart-protective compound found in red wine. Blueberries are frequently included on lists of the best "brain foods," and they make a great snack. Even kids like them.

3. **Eat whole wheat bread** — Switching to whole wheat bread is not hard. Supermarkets and delis usually carry it, and bakeries are producing more and more whole wheat options. Most bagel stores offer whole wheat bagels, and many have whole wheat "everything" bagels — which I get for my family, and which ended the complaints that I used to get from my kids when I got plain whole wheat. (By going for "everything," however, I'm adding salt.) You may not always find whole wheat rolls, so if you love your lunch sandwich on a roll, you may have to make a bit more of change to go for whole wheat bread, but it's worth it.

Be careful. Wheat bread is not the same as whole wheat bread. It's the whole grains that provide the health benefits. So make sure you are buying "whole" wheat. "Multi-grain" or "stone-ground" sound healthy, but unless they are also whole grain, they're not what you want to choose.

4. **Cut down on bread in general** — The low-carb craze that followed the introduction of the Atkins Diet, then the South Beach Diet, led many people to cut down on bread. You can make important progress in your eating habits by switching from bread-like snacks, such as cakes, cookies, and pretzels, to nuts, fruits, and even low-fat or no-fat ice cream or frozen (or nonfrozen) yogurt. Because I know this is asking a lot, I'm going to stretch out the implementation of this habit by breaking it down into several steps.

5. **Stop eating cookies (or drastically cut down)** — Cookies are a tough habit to break. They're so delicious (sugar and butter are two tasty ingredients) and when they're served at a party or business meeting, they're usually put out on a huge tray. If you do eat cookies, choose oatmeal cookies and limit your intake. Cake and pie fall into the same category as cookies. If you now eat them regularly, try to make them just special-occasion foods.

6. **Stop eating doughnuts** — Doughnuts are bad because they're deep-fried, loaded with sugar, and not made from whole grains. They're one of the most unhealthy foods. They were even worse before many stores stopped making them with trans fats (though some still may).

7. **Stop eating so many pretzels** — When the no-carbs craze was upon us, I embraced the idea of cutting out the empty calories from white flour. I didn't realize how much white flour I had been eating until I tried to cut back — and pretzels were one of the biggest culprits.

They were my No. 1 snack. We ate them at home all the time, and I kept a supply at my office. They seemed like the perfect snack because, unlike potato chips, they had no fat, which had previously been the focus of most health-media attention. I switched from pretzels to nuts — which have *good* fat.

8. **Eat almonds** — I keep a can in my car and a can in my office desk, and I eat an ounce or so a day as a mid-morning or mid-afternoon snack. Almonds are a much healthier snack than potato chips. I love Blue Diamond's roasted and salted variety. Whole natural almonds are better for you, but I like the roasted and salted ones better, and because I'm fortunate to have low blood pressure and I never add salt to my food, I don't worry about the salt. (It's tough to be perfect. It's easier to do these things if you are not too hard on yourself.)

9. **Eat brown rice, not white rice** — Ask for brown rice when you're at a restaurant or order takeout, and make brown rice at home. You can even order brown rice with your sushi. This is similar to switching from white bread to whole wheat.

10. **Eat whole grain pasta** — Supermarkets now carry various types of whole grain pasta, and I'm finding it at more and more restaurants. (You can also buy whole wheat pancake mix, and order whole wheat pancakes at many restaurants.)

11. **Eat whole grain cereals** — Whole grain cereals don't taste like cardboard. Many of them taste great. Like the salted almonds that I like, my favorite breakfast cereals would probably not be the top recommendations from nutritionists (too much sugar), but they are all made from whole grains. Marcie and I buy most of our cereals at Trader Joe's. We love their Trek Mix Granola (Antioxidant Nut & Berry Blend), though I mention this at the risk that it could be dis-

continued. (Trader Joe's adds new products regularly and discontinues ones that don't sell well — sometimes to my dismay, as I seem to like things they discontinue.) They have many more whole grain cereals to choose from. You have to read the nutrition label, though; Trader Joe's tends to have healthy choices, but it's not a health food store and you still want to check what's in each product. If you don't have a Trader Joe's near you, healthy brand-name cereals are available at regular supermarkets, and large supermarkets are carrying more and more non-name-brand selections, many of which are healthy choices. We eat Cheerios (or Honey Nut Cheerios or the Trader Joe's version, Joe's O's). Kudos to General Mills (the maker of Cheerios) for making all its cereals from whole grains. I also recommend that you Google "how to pick a breakfast cereal" to find Diana Mirkin's list of recommended cereals available at most supermarkets. I eat a cocktail of cereals each morning. I like the different tastes and textures. I also add walnuts and blueberries, as I mentioned earlier, and skim milk.

12. **Do not buy foods with artificial colors** — This is really part of a bigger habit — reading labels on the foods you buy. When I was a kid, we ate all the junky (delicious) cereals. Then my mom heard that artificial colors and preservatives should be avoided. She started to read food labels and quickly saw that the breakfast cereals we were eating (some of you who are my age may recall Quisp and Quake, for example) were loaded with artificial colors and preservatives. So we started eating Kellogg's Raisin Bran every day. I still like it and it makes Diana Mirkin's recommended list of cereals, mentioned above.

13. **Do not buy foods with partially hydrogenated oils** — I first read about this in Dr. Andrew Weil's 1997 book, *8 Weeks to Optimum Health*. Partially hydrogenated oils are the notorious trans fats that have deservedly received so much criticism during the past decade.

Thanks to all of the negative attention, many people now know about the importance of avoiding trans fats, and food manufacturers have been required to include trans fat content on food labels since 2006. The manufacturers have eliminated these fats from many products, and it's become common to see "no trans fats" advertised on packages. You should buy foods with 0g (zero grams) of trans fat. This will build on your habit of reading labels before you buy.

14. **Limit your total fat intake to 30 percent or less of your total daily calories** — Once again, you have to read labels. Fat content has been on food labels for quite a while — much longer than trans fats. And here you have to do a bit of math. For example, if a product contains 110 calories per serving, 10 of which are calories from fat, that's less than 10 percent fat calories. Conversely, if it's 110 calories, of which 80 are from fat, that's more than 70 percent fat calories. The American Heart Association has great information about fats on its Web site.

15. **Avoid saturated fats** — You should steer clear of animal fat, butter fat, and "tropical oils" — such as coconut oil, palm kernel oil, and palm oil. They are bad for your heart health. Your label-reading habit will serve you well here.

16. **Avoid cottonseed oil** — Cottonseed oil is a source of saturated fat. I'm giving it its own listing because of all the bad things I've read about it. Google "Why is cottonseed oil bad for you?" and keep a garbage can by your side in case you get sick reading about it. I moved away from one well-known brand of "cocktail peanuts" because it is made with "peanut and/or cottonseed oil" and switched to others that just use peanut oil.

17. **Drink skim milk** — As part of your fat-reduction plan, drink skim milk (also known as nonfat or fat-free milk). I drank tons of whole

milk as a child, until my mom read that skim milk is much healthier. Skim milk looked like milky water to us, and it tasted sour. So Mom broke us in slowly. We switched to 2 percent milk, then 1 percent, then finally skim milk. If you're a whole milk drinker, transition to skim milk with this three-step process and do it over 63 days (three 21-day habits). There's a good chance you can do it in 42 days or even in 21. Or try Skim Plus, which is what we drink in our house. I don't know how or why, but it has a thick, rich taste that is much closer to the taste of whole milk than that of ordinary skim milk. With that taste, you can easily move from whole milk to skim milk in 21 days. I find milk in my cereal to be refreshing — it really hits the spot to eat a bowl of cereal with milk for breakfast, right after I've exercised. (Note: I rarely drink milk otherwise, so the taste is not as important to me as it would be if I drank it by the glass. But I do have friends who are milk drinkers and swear by Skim Plus.)

18. **Do not put butter on your bread** — Per my earlier suggestion, eat less bread. When you do eat it, don't top it with butter, but instead use olive oil, avocado, hummus, or butter substitutes that do not contain partially hydrogenated oils/trans fats — or, for my super-radical suggestion, how about this: Eat the bread plain! Like so many people, I grew up buttering my bread. I simply don't do it anymore. When I order eggs in a restaurant, I order dry whole wheat toast. I also enjoy eating really good bread that tastes great without butter. (One funny story for those of you who think dry toast is unappealing: When my brother, who is a healthy eater, read a draft of this chapter, he commented that he wasn't enthusiastic about the idea of dry toast. When I went to pick up the copy of the chapter with his notes, he left it for me outside his front door so I wouldn't wake up his kids by ringing the doorbell. Along with the chapter I found a cup of crushed ice with this note: "Perhaps you'll enjoy this tasty new treat I've been eating lately instead of ice cream.")

19. **Do not eat foods with monosodium glutamate (MSG)** — I remember when we first heard about MSG. Health experts told us that when we eat at Chinese restaurants, we should ask that our food be made without MSG. Now, most Chinese restaurants have "No MSG" prominently displayed on menus and signs. Because I regularly read the labels on all the foods I buy, I occasionally notice monosodium glutamate and I put those products (usually soups) back on the shelf.

20. **Limit your intake of red meat** — When I was a kid, we ate hamburgers (with tater tots) for dinner every night, except maybe the one time a week we had chicken. As a treat, once in a while we had steak or lamb chops. Fish was not part of the equation until much later — so much later that I actually remember the first time I ate fish. Now I frequently eat fish. And I eat chicken all the time.

21. **Buy some organic foods** — Dr. Weil periodically publishes a list of fruits and vegetables that you should always buy organic. Google Dr. Weil to find the most recent version of this list. Regarding some of the items on his list:

    Marcie and I have been buying organic strawberries ever since I read years ago that strawberries are among the fruits that absorb the most pesticides. I love eating apples, and our supermarket almost always carries several organic varieties, at the same price as the "conventional" (non-organic) varieties. Organic spinach seems to be regularly available at the supermarkets near us, and baby spinach is our primary salad choice.

22. **Eat an apple a day** — I love apples. There are so many kinds that you are bound to find one you like. They're a great snack. They're sweet, so they satisfy the sugar craving. They're thirst-quenching. They're a good source of fiber. I keep them in the fridge, because I like them

cold and crisp. Marcie likes to keep them out on the counter, because she feels that our family won't eat them if they are "hidden away in the fridge, out of sight, out of mind." But once you get into the habit of eating one apple each day, you'll have no problem remembering them. I've gotten into the habit of bringing one with me to work almost every day. I enjoy eating them whole or cutting them into slices. When I used to hear my kids rummaging around the kitchen looking for a snack, I would offer to cut up a couple of apples — and all my kids grew to be fans of the fruit. I also packed sliced apples in their lunches (squirting a little lemon juice on them so they wouldn't turn brown in their lunch bags). And remember — buy them organic.

23. **Don't salt your food** — When I was on a bicycle tour as a teenager, a counselor saw one of my fellow teens salting his food and told us this story: My dad was once interviewing a young man for a job. As part of the interview, my dad took the job candidate out to lunch. As soon as their lunches arrived, the young man grabbed the salt shaker and shook salt into his soup. My dad ate his lunch, thanked the candidate for his time, and told the young man that he was not going to be receiving a job offer. "Why not?" asked the young man. "Because you salted your food before you tasted it. How did you know it needed salt if you hadn't tasted it yet?" I don't know if this is a true story, or an urban legend perpetuated by the counselor's dad to teach his son a life lesson. ("Think before you act, and don't act without having all the information you need to make a decision.") I looked it up on Snopes.com, a great site for checking the legitimacy of urban legends. Snopes reports that many famous executives are said to have used this mealtime test as part of their evaluation of job candidates, but Snopes cannot confirm that it was really done.

Either way, I've always remembered that story. When I heard it, I was proud that I would never find myself in that situation because I had stopped salting my food years earlier; my mom, in addition to imploring us to stop salting our food, had removed the salt shaker from its traditional spot on the kitchen table. I continue that practice today. My kids would never expect to see a salt shaker on a kitchen or dining room table. Like so many other habits (drinking skim milk, not buttering your bread), eliminating the use of the salt shaker is something you will get used to — and soon enough you'll find out how delicious foods are without the extra salt. Corn on the cob, for instance. We grew up eating corn by rolling it in butter and then salting it. There's no doubt that it tastes delicious that way. But good corn tastes great without the butter and salt. It's like a different food — different, but still delicious. Salt has long been known to increase your blood pressure, which is why people with high blood pressure are told to minimize their salt intake. It's especially important not to *add* salt to food because there is *already* so much salt in so much of what we eat. And I hope the story about my counselor's dad will cause you to pause before repeating some of your other eating habits, like automatically adding mayo to sandwiches before you've even taken a bite.

24. **Eat sweet potatoes, not white potatoes** — We all have automatic eating habits, including avoiding certain foods — sometimes for no good reason. For example, until I was about 40 years old, I thought I didn't like sweet potatoes. Then someone urged me try some at a family holiday gathering, and they were awesome. (I think there were marshmallows melted on top, which didn't hurt.) Soon after that, I heard that white potatoes weren't a great food choice and that sweet potatoes were more healthful — so at my house, we started making sweet potatoes a regular part of our diet.

25. **Don't eat French fries** — French fries, despite their name, seem as American as apple pie. You can find them everywhere, from diners

to McDonald's to country fairs to sporting events. At my home, we eat sweet potato "fries" all the time. But they're not fried. We cut the sweet potatoes into the size of steak fries, put them on a pan with light olive oil and some spices, and bake them. They're fantastic. We practically fight over them at the dinner table.

26. **Don't eat chicken skin** — We peel the skin off the chicken before we cook it. Chicken skin is fat — and not the good kind. It's a bit of a hassle, but worth the effort. (Make sure you always clean your hands and the work surface thoroughly after handling raw chicken.) If you don't peel the chicken before cooking it, or if you're not the one doing the cooking, peel the skin off the cooked chicken before you eat it.

27. **Eat chicken grilled or roasted, not fried** — Fried chicken also seems as American as apple pie, but it's high on the list of foods you should eliminate from your diet. The batter soaks up lots of oil from the deep fryer, so you end up ingesting a large dose of fat. There are much better ways of eating chicken. Roasted and grilled chickens are delicious.

28. **Avoid all deep-fried foods** — The WebMD article titled "10 Foods That are Health Horrors" has deep-fried foods at the top of the list. Enough said.

29. **Eat salmon** — Many people don't like fish. "It tastes too fishy," they say. But salmon is a pretty mild-flavored fish and it's a great source of omega-3 fatty acids, which are highly recommended for their health benefits. In fact, your doctor may have recommended taking fish oil pills as a supplement. My family enjoys cooking salmon or eating it in restaurants, and we also buy salmon in a can (the same way you buy tuna fish in a can). Wild Alaskan salmon in a can (as opposed to farm-raised salmon, which you should avoid) seems to be widely available in supermarkets, and that's a good thing. While salmon is

high on the list of fish that are good for your health, there are many other excellent fish choices. Make sure that you incorporate fish into your diet as a heart-healthy alternative to red meat.

30. **Avoid fish with too much mercury** — This is a health issue that has received increasing attention in recent years. The Web site gotmercury.org will help you calculate the mercury content in the fish you eat.

31. **Do not eat the skin of fish** — As with chicken, it's best to remove skin from fish before you cook it. The skin is fatty and pollutants accumulate there.

32. **Eat fruit** — Fruit is nature's dessert. It's sweet, it's delicious, and it's good for you. Yes, we eat "traditional dessert" in our house, but we also eat fruit. Lots of it. Perhaps if you serve fruit at dessert time, you'll eat less ice cream and other more fattening desserts. And even if it doesn't help you cut down on other desserts, you'll benefit from eating fruit, which contains important vitamins, minerals, and fiber.

33. **Eat vegetables** — This goes without saying, but, then again, it has to be said. Vegetables, along with fruit, have always been considered one of the key foods to eat for a healthy you. "Eat your vegetables, they're good for you" is not an old wives' tale. Your mom was right about this one.

34. **Eat lots of fiber** — Fiber is a key to colon health, and is obtained from fruits, vegetables, whole grains, seeds, and nuts. According to Dr. Mehmet C. Oz and Dr. Michael F. Roizen's *You, The Owner's Manual*, lima beans, artichokes, soybeans, almonds, peanuts, oatmeal, buckwheat cereal, and some other breakfast cereals are good, quick sources of fiber. For this 21-day habit, add something more to

what you've already been eating in these categories — at least one additional fiber-rich food every day.

35. **Eat salad** — Whether you eat at home or out, salad is a pretty common appetizer, and that's a good thing. Salads are a great way to get vegetables into your diet. I eat a salad at lunch or dinner (or both) every day. And it's easy to include salad in your meals even if you feel that you don't have time for preparation, because today you can buy many types of washed, cut, ready-to-eat salads at the store.

36. **Eat spinach** — I have long heard that spinach has more nutritional value than iceberg lettuce. I never bothered to look up this information until now. In 1998, Texas A&M University published a study comparing the nutrient content of different types of spinach and lettuce, and the results were clear. Spinach wins. Your mom and Popeye were right. If your family is used to eating iceberg, and you are concerned about their willingness to give it up, I suggest a gradual transition (similar to my suggested approach for switching to skim milk). Move from iceberg alone to mostly iceberg with some baby spinach mixed in, to half and half, to mostly spinach with iceberg mixed in. I also highly recommend sautéed spinach with garlic and olive oil. It's one of my favorite foods, at home and at restaurants, and the garlic and olive oil are good for you too.

37. **Do not pour salad dressing directly onto your food** — It's amazing how much more dressing most of us put on our salad when pouring it straight from the bottle. My wife taught me this trick: Pour the salad dressing into the cap, and then pour that onto your food. It makes it a bit messy when you screw the cap back on, but that can be remedied by rinsing it off. In restaurants, ask them to go light on the dressing, or ask for the dressing on the side.

38. **Avoid creamy dressings** — Olive oil is a much healthier fat than those in creamy salad dressings such as ranch and blue cheese. I know you may like those, but vinaigrette and similar dressings are tasty too. If you try and fail at adopting this suggestion, go back one habit and at least use less dressing by measuring a small portion before putting it on the salad. Another way to use less dressing is to dip the salad into the dressing. When you order dressing on the side, you'll be amazed how much is left in the bowl when you eat it using the dip method.

39. **Avoid creamy dips** — Like creamy dressing, creamy dips and sour cream are full of the bad fats and should be avoided. Try black bean dips or hummus. Or how about this: Try eating vegetables plain! Carrots are delicious. You don't need to dip them. When I was a kid, I loved eating potato chips with dip. Now, both parts of that snack are a total turnoff to me. The greasy potato chips. The creamy dip. Too rich for my taste. It's amazing that such a combo was invented — as if chips aren't tasty enough, we need to add dip? I do understand, though. As I said, I ate it as a kid. And in college one of my favorite snacks was cheddar fries at Sutter's across the street from the Albany State campus. Cheddar fries are French fries with melted cheddar poured on top. Heart attack on a plate. Sutter's is still there and at a recent reunion I ordered sweet potato fries, a relatively recent addition to their menu. I knew I was ordering deep-fried food. I indulge sometimes. A friend ordered cheddar fries. I tried a couple and found I had lost my taste for them. That happens, for sure.

40. **Cut down on cheese made from whole milk** — As an extension of the recommendation to switch from whole milk to nonfat (aka skim) milk, you should also switch to low-fat cheese wherever possible or cut down on your use of cheese made from whole milk. For example, avoid cream cheese. It's heavy in the bad type of fat.

If you're going to use it, make sure you spread it on thin. Cream cheese has a lot of flavor and you'll see how quickly you'll find that a thin "schmear" is all you need to enjoy it. And give some thought to your consumption of pizza. I used to think that pizza was the perfect food. Bread, protein, and vegetable. Then I cut way back on cheese. Then I cut way back on bread. Pizza took a big hit. Pizza is delicious but shouldn't be eaten many times each week, as I used to do. You can now get pizza with whole wheat dough in some places, as well as with low-fat cheese. If you make it at home, some frozen varieties have those healthier ingredients, or you can buy whole wheat pizza dough in many supermarkets to create your own "healthy" pizza.

41. **Eat yogurt** — This is one of my later-in-life finds. I always thought I didn't like yogurt. I didn't like it when I tried it many years ago — I thought it tasted sour — and that was that. Over the ensuing years, I heard so many good things about yogurt, but I never considered trying it again. Then, one day in 2006 or so, I was stuck in an airport for a prolonged delay. I had already eaten breakfast at home and wanted a snack. I saw those delicious pretzels they dip in a buttery sauce, I saw those gigantic cinnamon buns (heart attack in a bag), and I saw a variety of packaged foods at a coffee place. I picked up a yogurt container, eyed it warily, and thought of my 80-plus-year-old friend Jim, whom I told you about in the last chapter. Jim is one of the smartest, youngest-for-his-age people I've ever met. I thought about all those times I saw him eating yogurt in the lunchroom when we worked together. So I tried it. It was nonfat peach yogurt. And it was excellent. It hit the spot. Yes, it had that sour taste that yogurt tends to have, but it didn't offend my taste buds the way it did when I was a kid. When I got home, I started trying different types of yogurt. It was easy because my wife usually keeps yogurt in the house. I found a few kinds I liked and have been eating it ever since.

One more thing about yogurt: It's an incredibly convenient snack, and that's valuable. The single-serving containers are easy to take with you from home, and when you're away from home, you can find it at almost any food store.

42. **Eat slowly** — My dad has always had more energy than anyone I've ever met and probably more than anyone most people have ever met. The energy is evident in the way he moves, the amount he accomplishes every day, and pretty much everything about him. But he eats incredibly slowly. If he's eating with a group, he's always the last one to finish. When I was a kid, I used to wolf down my food — I would eat half a pie of pizza in five minutes — and my dad would always tell me to slow down. He would tell me to chew 25 times before swallowing, which seemed impossible. I still don't eat as slowly as my dad does, but I do eat much more slowly than I did as a kid. It took a conscious effort to make that happen.

There are many reasons to eat slowly. First, you enjoy your food more. Why not make it last longer if you're enjoying it? Second, you will probably eat less by eating more slowly. If you eat quickly, by the time your stomach tells you that you've had enough, you will already have had more than enough. Why do you think those hot-dog-eating contestants eat so fast? Yes, their goal is to eat as many as they can as fast as they can, but there's also no way they could eat as much as they do if they ate slowly (check out Paul Newman's struggle to eat hard-boiled eggs in *Cool Hand Luke*).

In addition to thoroughly chewing your food, put down your fork and knife between each bite. Chew. Swallow. Then pick up your utensils to move on to the next forkful. It's a great habit. You'll enjoy your meal more, you'll be healthier, and you'll look more civilized. (I'm speaking from personal experience; my own eating etiquette used to be horrible. It has changed dramatically from what it used to be, and it took years for me to improve those habits, one change at a time.)

43. **Eat dark chocolate** — Most people love this recommendation. Dark chocolate, which contains antioxidants, is widely viewed these days as being good for your health, as long as you don't overindulge. Choose dark chocolate with at least 70 percent cocoa. There are many types of dark chocolate, and you can have a lot of fun finding the ones you like best. Dark chocolate with high cocoa content can be bitter, so sample a few different ones. WebMD recommends eating a small amount of dark chocolate every day, for a total of about one chocolate bar each week. "Gourmet" brands of dark chocolate can be expensive, but I have found several reasonably priced varieties that I like.

44. **Do not drink soda** — Like almost every kid on the planet, I learned to love soda at an early age. I drank everything: Coke, Pepsi, 7 Up, Sprite, Mountain Dew, orange soda. Riding my bike into town for two slices of pizza and a cup of soda at Pioneer Pizza on a Saturday afternoon — that was the life. My kids love soda, but they almost never get to drink it at home. We drink seltzer with a splash of juice (during my son's high school years, his was closer to juice with a splash of seltzer). I love seltzer with a splash of orange juice or grapefruit juice. I also enjoy it with grape juice, and because grape juice (like its cousin red wine) is believed to be good for you, that's a good choice. My wife likes seltzer with a *splash* of cranberry juice. Note that I am recommending just a splash because juice contains a lot of sugar. (It takes almost a pound of oranges to produce eight ounces of juice, so those eight ounces contain five to eight teaspoons of sugar.) When you do buy juice, make sure it's 100 percent juice, not "juice drink," which may contain just a small percentage of real fruit juice. Read those labels!

45. **Drink water** — It's hard to get into the habit of drinking eight glasses of water a day, as is widely recommended by health experts. But I've read a few things that made me feel better about the amount of water I drink. I learned that the water you get from eating foods that contain water, such as fresh fruits and vegetables, counts toward the eight-glasses-a-day quota. If you drink at meals and when you feel thirsty, that's going to be pretty close to the right amount for you. (Drinking when you're thirsty may sound like something that everyone does automatically, but it's actually a habit that many people have to work on. I know there are many times when I'm sitting at my desk feeling thirsty but I put off getting a drink, and then suddenly I realize that a couple of hours have passed.) One indicator of whether you're taking in enough water can be checked when you go to the bathroom: If your urine is bright yellow, you should be drinking more.

46. **Drink red wine** — Almost all the sources I've read on the health benefits of foods and drinks recommend red wine. For the many people who already enjoy red wine, this has been wonderful news, and for those of you who are not yet red wine drinkers, I don't blame you if you choose this as one of your first habits to adopt. Red grape juice has similar benefits without the alcohol.

47. **Drink green tea** — This is another widely recommended habit. For many years, my wife has made herbal iced tea, which we keep in our fridge. She throws a bunch of herbal tea bags into a container along with hot water. After the bags have steeped for a while, she adds cold water and then refrigerates it. In order to get the benefits of green tea, she's been adding green tea bags to the mix. And sometimes she adds some honey to enhance the flavor. My son and all his teenage friends love it. They call it "Mrs. Singa's Famous." It really hits the spot, and as I write about it I have the urge to get up and get some.

There are many flavorful herbal iced teas available, and you can get decaffeinated green tea if you prefer that (as we do).

48. **Eat tomato products** — When you eat tomatoes, especially when they're cooked, you benefit from lycopene, which is touted as reducing the risk of prostate cancer. Prostate cancer has gotten a lot of publicity lately because of its increased incidence, which may be due, in part, to the increase in men's longevity. (The publicity is also attributable to the fact that many famous men — Joe Torre, Rudy Giuliani, Nelson Mandela, and Arnold Palmer, among others — have been treated for and have survived prostate cancer.) Ketchup makers have begun to advertise the lycopene benefit (because ketchup is made from cooked tomatoes), and I've eaten more ketchup since learning of it. Tomato sauce is also an easy way for people to get their lycopene.

49. **Eat watermelon** — I learned relatively recently that watermelon is also a source of lycopene. I had thought that watermelon, being mostly water and sugar, had little nutritional value. A good, sweet watermelon is one of the most wonderful foods, delicious and refreshing, so I was happy to hear that it has important health benefits.

50. **Eat edamame** — I first tried edamame (soybeans that are cooked and served in the pod) when eating Japanese food with a Japanese friend in Manhattan. I was amazed that after many years of eating Japanese food, I had never had edamame. It's available in almost all Japanese restaurants and can be bought frozen in many grocery stores to be prepared at home. Many Japanese restaurants now offer edamame on the table in the same way other restaurants offer a basket of bread. I wish all restaurants did that! Edamame is tasty (in part because of the salt that's added), high in protein, and fun to eat — you squeeze the beans out of the pod into your mouth.

51. **Avoid nitrates and nitrites** — Stay away from these preservatives. Look for them when you are reading the labels of dried fruit and cured meats.

52. **Eat beans** — Beans appear on many lists of the healthiest foods. Marcie and I have always eaten a good amount of them. Mexican food makes great use of beans — a whole wheat burrito with beans, brown rice, salad, avocado, and some low-fat cheese makes a great, healthy meal. Black bean soup is delicious, as is minestrone soups, which is usually made with some type of bean.

✳ Keeping Track of Your Progress

Those are my 52 recommended healthy eating habits. As you strive to adopt the new habits, keep a journal to track your progress. It can be as simple as a plain notebook with one page for each 21-day period. For example, as each 21-day cycle begins, write the numbers 1-21 down the left side of a new page, and then at the end of each day check off a number and add any notes you want to remember. I write down everything because (as we discussed in Chapter 4, Be Organized) it helps to keep me on track in all parts of my life.

As you go through the 52 habits, check them off in this book. If you already have some of the habits, check them off now and simply consider yourself ahead of the game. Don't use them as 21-day free passes. Build some momentum and don't stop. If you start with some habits checked off or you adopt some habits in fewer than 21 days, or both, and consequently it takes you only two years to get through the 52, then wonderful. Use the third year to add 17 or so additional good habits.

Remember, you can make the 52 eating changes in any order you wish. And keeping in mind our Chapter 4 discussion regarding eating the big frog first, you may wish to start with the ones you consider the most challenging. After the challenging ones, the other ones will seem easy. Alternatively, start with an easy one if you feel it will help you get on a roll.

All of this change, even broken down into 52 bite-size pieces, may feel daunting to you. You may say to yourself, "How am I going to incorporate so many new habits?" Don't do that. Don't look forward, except to set your goals. Instead, imagine yourself three years from now and feel how great it is to have accomplished all these goals. It's an incredibly satisfying feeling. Thinking about your achievements is a good thing to do in general (in Chapter 1 I suggested doing it at the end of each day), so throughout the three years, keep looking back at your progress. It will feel good each time you take stock of all the changes you've made. As we all know, three years goes by in the blink of an eye. Imagine how much more fulfilled you'll be three years from now after you've made so many positive changes in your life. You'll be happier knowing how much longer you're likely to live because of your 52 improvements. You'll feel better physically and mentally, you'll have a better outlook on the future, and you'll look better.

Feel free to substitute other habits for those on the list. There are many places to find good habits to add: things you read; things a friend tells you; things a doctor recommends. There will also be health-related discoveries over the three years and it's important that you stay up-to-date. Some of the information sources that I look at regularly are: Dr. Weil's e-mail newsletter, Real Age's e-mail newsletter, WebMD's e-mail newsletter, *Prevention* magazine and their e-mail newsletters, and the *New York Times* Science Times section on Tuesdays. New trends are usually picked up by all of these publications around the same time.

Dr. Weil has been a guru of good health for decades. I learned about him by reading his books, including *8 Weeks to Optimum Health* and *Eating*

Well for Optimum Health. I know we're all inundated with e-mails, and I recommend that you unsubscribe from e-mail newsletters that you don't look at, but I strongly suggest that you visit Dr. Weil's Web site and register for his e-mails. You'll learn a lot and you'll stay on top of the latest health news. He also has his own version of the food pyramid — the only food pyramid I've seen that includes dark chocolate and red wine. WebMD has similar resources, and in the *New York Times* Science Times I particularly like the columns by Jane Brody and Tara Parker-Pope.

✳ You Need to Change Your Eating Habits. And You Can.

Do you drink coffee? Did you like it the first time you tried it? Did you hear, "It's an acquired taste"? It takes time to develop the taste for many foods, particularly foods that are good for you. When you switch from white bread to whole wheat, it may take some getting used to. Same thing when you switch from whole milk to nonfat milk (skim milk). If you smoke, and I hope you don't, did you like that first cigarette? I bet you didn't. Another acquired taste. You worked at it. At some point you grew to like the cigarettes. If you were willing to work at smoking, aren't you willing to work at acquiring the taste for foods that are good for you? And I'm not talking about foods that taste bad. I'm just talking about foods that are often not as rich, sweet, or salty as the foods we normally find so appealing.

Be patient. Don't try to short-cut the process. I didn't adopt all of these 52 eating habits over three years. I was in my early teens when my mother switched us to skim milk because she had read that the fat in whole milk could clog our arteries. A bit earlier, she had told us we couldn't eat junky cereals any longer because they had artificial colors and preservatives like BHA and BHT, which she worried might cause cancer. Later, she introduced us to fish for dinner instead of the hamburgers we had been eating most nights because too much red meat was bad for your heart. Then we learned that eating too many egg yolks was bad (causing high levels of something called cholesterol, which we had never heard of). She stopped putting a salt shaker on the dinner table because salt was bad for your blood pressure. So as I grew up I learned the habits of watching what I ate, paying attention to nutritional news, and reading labels on food packages.

And my kids learned to do the same. They grew up in the era when we discovered the dangers of trans fats. From an early age, they were checking food labels for partially hydrogenated oils. Like most kids, they wanted to help out at the supermarket. I would grab the can or bottle or bag or box off the shelf and they would say, "Daddy, let me look." If they found partially hydrogenated oil, they put it back; otherwise, they would tell me the product was okay.

What you're going to be doing is not just for yourself, but also for everyone you live with. My kids learned from me and I learned from my mother. By teaching your kids how to eat right, you'll be teaching your grandchildren how to eat right.

If undertaking one of the well-known diets I listed earlier helps you to eat better, great. Just find something that works for you because eating well is one of the key components of being healthy.

The 52 habits I listed are not a short-term fix. Although I talk about making these 52 changes over a three-year period, this isn't a three-year diet. These are lifestyle changes for your entire lifetime. It's a lifetime diet. And while it may help you lose weight — eating better is an important part of any weight-loss program, along with eating less and exercising — it's not about losing weight. This is a "be healthy" diet. So I'm going to call it that: "The *Be Healthy* Diet." Jane Brody has written over and over about the fundamentals of maintaining a healthy diet. In one of her New Year's Day columns, she summed up the gold standard of a wholesome diet as one with meals made up of vegetables, fruits, whole grains, and a small serving of a protein-rich food.

I love how she keeps it simple. It bears repeating. Meals with vegetables, fruits, whole grains, and a small serving of a protein-rich food are the gold standard of a wholesome diet.

One thing I did not get into here is how much and how often you should eat various foods. Experts' recommendations tend to fluctuate over time, and you can look them up easily. More important, I didn't want to harp on specific numbers because achieving those targets, every week, all year, for every category, can be difficult. As is true in most areas of our lives, perfectionism isn't necessary. In fact, it can be a hindrance. Many people try to do something perfectly, but then if they can't, they give up the effort completely. That doesn't get you anywhere. Instead, make small changes and slowly build on them. In an excellent article in *Prevention* titled "You Don't Need to Be a Health Perfectionist," Camille Noe Pagan wrote about some of the strategies for getting fit. What I loved is that she provided not just the "gold standard" recommendations for diet and exercise, but also corresponding "good enough guidelines" that will still help you make progress. For example, for fruits and vegetables, the gold standard is up to nine servings of fruits and vegetables a day, but it's "good enough" to have five a day. For portion sizes, the gold standard is to measure everything you eat, but her "good enough" suggestion is to measure grains and fats only.

One way to add to your list of ideas for healthful lifestyle changes is to find out your RealAge® and learn some recommendations for bringing down your RealAge. RealAge is an invention of Dr. Roizen and Dr. Oz, authors of the aforementioned *You, The Owner's Manual* and other books. Your RealAge is not how many years you've been alive, but how "old" your body is based on your lifestyle and a variety of health factors. Go to RealAge.com and take the free test. I took it when my calendar age was 44 and was told that my RealAge was only 31.5. Then they provided recommendations for further reducing my RealAge, such as flossing my teeth. I had never gotten into the habit of flossing, despite many dentists and hygienists imploring me to do so for most of my life. But when I read it on my RealAge report, it finally got me started, and in about 21 days my habit was formed.

Roizen and Oz's *You* titles have been health-book sensations. They're easy to read and have fun illustrations. Two of my favorite parts of *You, The Owner's Manual* are "The Owner's Manual Diet Basics: Crib Sheet" and an exercise crib sheet. The diet basics crib sheet has guidelines for meal schedules; portion sizes; which foods to eat daily three times a week, and weekly; which foods to avoid; what to drink every day; and what vitamins and supplements to take daily.

Be Healthy, Part 2: Exercise

Everyone knows that exercise is super-important. Yet, as we've discussed, many people have difficulty maintaining an exercise regimen. Exercise is even more important than eating well. If you eat really well, but you never exercise, your heart will give out sooner than it should. On the other hand, exercise can overcome a lot of the negatives from eating poorly. A study published in *The Journal of the American Medical Association* found that fitness level was the strongest predictor of death rates. Even people who had a minimal level of fitness had half the risk of dying as those who were least fit.

Eating well and exercise are *both* challenging for most of us. It's hard to say which is more challenging. Exercise is more challenging for many people because it's strictly about start behaviors, whereas eating has starts, stops, and changes. For example, in my eating recommendations, I've asked you to start eating certain foods, to stop eating certain foods, and to make certain changes to the way you eat. With exercise, it's all about starting, or doing more. With eating, I can tell you to go to the supermarket and buy this and that. You're going to eat anyway, so it's a matter of what products you choose. But I can't tell you to go to the supermarket and buy exercise. You have to *do* it. (Even if there were a pill that gave you some of the benefits of exercise — which might be available someday — actual exercise would undoubtedly still be better for you, just as it's better to get your vitamins from food than from pills.)

I wish I could limit my exercise advice to Nike's simple "Just Do It," but I know that doesn't cut it for most of us. Just doing it is much easier said than done for many reasons: you need to make time to exercise; weather can impact your ability to exercise outside; equipment is needed for many exercises; and gym memberships are not free. Eating well is challenging, but you don't have to make the time to eat well, because you're already eating; the weather will rarely impact your ability to eat well; you don't need special equipment (the same knives, forks, and spoons that help you consume red meat, French fries, and cheese dip do just fine on fruits and vegetables); and you're already spending money on food whether or not you're eating well.

What both goals have in common is that they boil down to an attitude. A desire. You have to want the benefits of exercise badly enough to overcome the obstacles to creating the exercise habit.

✳ My Dad's Lucky Break

In 1994, we had a very icy winter. My dad, who was about 60, slipped on the ice and badly broke his leg. He had surgery to insert pins and plates, was laid up for months, and then did physical therapy to rehabilitate his leg. As part of the rehab, he had to walk on a treadmill. From that point on, he became a regular exerciser. He and my mom are still religious about exercise. They belong to a gym and exercise every day. It's bizarre to say, but that broken leg was the best thing that could have happened to him. It's going to add many years to his life.

My dad had already gotten a bit of a health wake-up years earlier when he was told that he had high cholesterol. He modified his diet and was told to exercise. But he didn't fully appreciate the importance of exercise — how good it would be for his cholesterol. Now, doctors are more likely to be more forceful when they recommend exercise. It was only in 2007 that the American College of Sports Medicine and the American Medical Association (AMA) announced *Exercise is Medicine*™, a program designed to encourage Americans to incorporate physical activity and exercise into their daily routine by calling on doctors to prescribe exercise to their patients.

In this book's introduction, I discussed kaizen, the process of constantly making small improvements. In the 1980s, I read *Kaizen: The Key to Japan's Competitive Success*, a book by Masaaki Imai. It left a great impression on me and influenced every aspect of my life, particularly at my office where my constant striving for improvements, even small ones, sometimes elicited less-than-enthusiastic responses ("We have to change this again? We just changed it last week."). The book on kaizen helped me explain to my colleagues all the good we were doing by implementing continuous improvement.

In 2004, I read *One Small Step Can Change Your Life: The Kaizen Way*, by Robert Maurer, PhD. In this wonderful book, which helps you achieve all types of changes in your life, Dr. Maurer provides a seemingly radical suggestion for the many people who can't seem to get started on an exercise routine: Start with a goal as tiny as one minute a day, building from there. This fits right in with my three-year eating program. How about this: Start by doing some form of exercise, no matter how seemingly insignificant, for one minute a day. Do that for 21 days. Then, do two minutes a day for 21 days. Then, three minutes. And so on. After three years (52 three-week periods), you'll be exercising for 52 minutes a day. That's pretty great. (More likely, at some point you'll end up choosing to increase your exercise period by more than one minute, but you don't have to.) Instead of overreaching, as with a New Year's resolution that's destined to fail, you're setting an achievable goal, and that's a good thing. A really good thing.

✳ How I Got Started With Exercise

I exercise for about an hour each day. Although my routine wasn't developed over 52 three-week periods, it did evolve via the major feature of my three-year, kaizen-inspired approach: continuous improvement.

Once again, I'm going to point to the influence of a career and life mentor of mine, Alan Mathog. I started exercising in 1987 when I was working with Alan. Alan preaches daily exercise and he put his money where his mouth is, building a gym in his office for his company's employees.

Inspired by Alan, my wife and I bought an exercise bike the winter I met Alan, and I started using it at night when I got home from work. It's a simple machine and I still have it. (I find that the more basic the machine, the longer it is likely to last.) It's completely nonelectric. I just sit down, crank the built-in timer (an old-fashioned device similar to a kitchen timer), turn up the resistance, and pedal.

In 1987, I had heard that 20 minutes a day was recommended, so that's what I did. Later, I read that you need to get your heart rate up for 20 minutes, so I upped the time on the bike to 30 minutes — a five-minute warm up at low resistance, 20 minutes at higher resistance, and a five-minute cool-down at almost no resistance.

My wife hated riding the bike and about five years later we bought a treadmill. Nothing fancy, no programs. Just one button for speed and another for elevation.

✳ How I Kept With It

I had tried running on treadmills in hotel gyms a few times and found it to be extremely boring, so I was in no rush to get on our new treadmill. Riding the exercise bike was boring as well, but I had developed a routine: reading while riding. I had no shortage of reading material from work. I never seemed to be able to get through it. I had developed the habit of creating a giant pile of the stuff, and the pile haunted me. "Read me," it said, over and over. That reading is an important activity for me to keep up and to learn new things. The reading helped pass the time on the bike, and time on the bike helped me get through my reading — so it was a double win. As the years went on, I started reading all sorts of material on the bike, and now it's mostly books.

With the treadmill taking up more than half of our exercise room (I use that term liberally to refer to the right side of our old laundry room), I decided to give it a try. I started slowly, so that I could try to read while walking. Over time, I worked my way up to 4.3 miles per hour while reading. I also began with a low elevation, setting it to 1 percent, and now I set it at 4 percent. I found that I enjoyed the treadmill, and I went from using it periodically to alternating daily between walking on the treadmill and riding the bike. My secret to reading on the treadmill is that I don't use a rack to hold the reading material. I hold it in my hands. I think that because the book moves with me, I don't get dizzy — and I don't lose my place. I'm no scientist, but that seems logical to me. That said, use caution if you start a reading-while-treadmilling routine. Make sure you use the safety strap that turns off the machine if you fall (I always use it).

I know I could be getting a more intense workout if I weren't reading, but I've made that sacrifice, as with other compromises I've made, to help me enjoy the exercise more — which, in turn, has helped me stick with exercising. In a good column in *Prevention*, fitness expert Chris Freytag endorses multitasking as a way to fit in exercise — for example, doing squats while you brush your teeth or doing heel raises while waiting in line.

✳ Exercise Every Morning

In the same way that *write down everything* is one of my mantras for being organized, *exercise every morning* is something I feel strongly about. Having kids got me into the morning habit because it became increasingly challenging to fit in exercise in the evening. When my son was a newborn, I was waking up for the 5 am feeding, after which I would rock him back to sleep. One morning, I realized that I could ride the exercise bike while reading and pushing his stroller back and forth. When he started to sleep later, I wanted to keep waking up early to exercise. It wasn't easy. Many mornings I had to push myself to get out of bed with a phrase I once heard: "Mind over mattress."

✳ Stretching

From the beginning, I did several leg stretches both before and after my bike and treadmill sessions. Over the years, I incorporated more and more stretches into my routine, in two ways.

The first was the result of an injury. In 1994, we bought a minivan. The instruction manual made it clear how easy it was to remove the seats, including the three-seat back bench. It's reasonably heavy, but more important, it's awkwardly shaped, and the manual should have advised people not to lift it themselves (at least people my size). Something didn't feel right when I lifted it, and later that day I felt pain in my lower back. The next day, while driving, I felt a shooting pain in my left leg. A couple of days later, I went to a physical therapist who treated me and gave me some exercises to do. I've had on-and-off back pain since the minivan incident, and I've tried to be much more careful about what things I lift and how I lift them (bend your knees, not your back). Each time I have back pain, I step up the frequency of the stretches, doing them multiple times each day. When I feel the need, I go to the physical therapist, who often teaches me new stretches.

Over the years, I added more and more stretches to what became my daily, morning stretching routine. Then, in 2000, after being urged many times by my sister-in-law, Michey, I tried a yoga class. I loved it. I felt so good physically and so relaxed after doing it that I started to attend regularly. I wasn't very good at it, but the teacher, Rama, encouraged me, and told me that if I kept at it for 10 years, my body would be 10 years younger than it was when I started (I started at age 38, and after doing it for 10 years, my 48-year-old body would be like the body of a 28-year-old). I quickly became hooked on yoga, attending up to three classes a week. On the days I wasn't able to attend, I did a mini-session on my own at home.

In June 2001, my wife and kids bought me a three-pack of yoga videos for Father's Day (*Power Yoga for Beginners 3-Pack: Stamina / Strength / Flexibility* with Rodney Yee). I tried it that summer, and by the end of the year I was doing yoga videos more often than going to yoga classes. The videos were only 20 minutes long, and not nearly as complete a workout or relaxation experience, but they were really good, and I got very good at the poses by doing yoga so often. By the end of 2002 I was hardly ever going to yoga classes. With kids at home, it was easier to fit in the time to do the videos in the morning at home — I could do shorter workouts, I could do them at my convenience, and I cut out the drive to the classes.

As time went on, I stopped using the yoga videos, but I developed a 15-minute stretching routine that I do before I get on the bike or the treadmill each day.

✳ Weight Training

At the end of 2002 I started working out with weights. I had done a little bit of weight training many years earlier during college when Glenn, a long-time weight trainer I was living with, started bringing me with him to the gym. It was fun to work out together. He taught me which exercises to do and how to do them, and we "spotted" each other. We went regularly for about a month and I started to notice a change in my physique, but then we went home for winter break for a month. When we came back, I let it drop. There was no good reason why I stopped, and as I write this I'm realizing that the memory of that experience helped me stick with my exercise-bike routine in the early years — I often *made* myself exercise because I worried that if I skipped a day I might stop doing it.

For years, I had known that weight training was an important missing element in my workouts. In the middle of 2001, I asked a friend of mine, the health and fitness expert Tony D'Assisi, for a few exercises to do if my goal was to be toned and fit, not to be the next Arnold Schwarzenegger. He gave me a list and urged me to arrange for a professional trainer to show me how to do the exercises correctly (not him, because he and I live many hours apart).

A year-and-a-half later, I decided to do something about it. Because working out at home had produced my greatest exercise success, I decided to get a home gym. Due to limited space, as well as my limited ambitions, I searched for the most basic one I could find. After buying it, I had trouble getting started. Months went by until three things happened in one week to get me going. First, my friend Mark asked whether I had been regularly using the machine. When I said I hadn't touched it yet, he laughed, amazed that I had joined the ranks of owners of idle home exercise equipment. He asked whether I was using it as a clothing rack. Then, my brother and sister-in-law, who a few weeks earlier had given me a session with a trainer as a birthday gift, asked me whether I had scheduled the session. Finally, a few days later, I was having lunch with Don, a wonderful friend about 15 years my senior. Don and I were talking about our workouts, and he was telling me how much he enjoyed listening to music while he worked out. That night, I grabbed a few CDs and one of our family's boom boxes and set them up by the weight machine.

The next morning I tried it — and I loved it. Like reading while exercising, which I had previously discovered, music and weight lifting were a match made in exercise heaven for me. I always long for more time to listen to music (or to read), so this routine was a win-win, and it got me rolling. I bought weight-lifting gloves to avoid blisters and scheduled time with the personal trainer. I've been working with weights about three times a week ever since.

I didn't follow through with all the exercises that Tony recommended — he gave me eight or 10 and I've been doing five. I do squats with a pair of free weights and three exercises on the machine: chest presses, seated rows, and lat pull-downs. I also do curls because I always wanted my biceps to look a bit more like Popeye's — they had always looked more like Olive Oyl's.

The personal trainer made sure I was doing the exercises correctly (I hadn't been). He also told me to do the reps slowly and put me on a routine of three sets of 12 reps for each of the exercises, with rest between the sets, which is important in weight lifting. I "circuit" through the five exercises, which provides the needed rest between each set.

✳ The Best Drug

Exercise is like a drug. Exercise is the fountain of youth everyone has been looking for. It helps your heart, your muscles, your bones, your mind, your energy level — pretty much every part of you. According to most sources, exercise reduces your risk for heart disease, cancer, Alzheimer's, stroke, diabetes, and depression.

I read in the *Wall Street Journal* that 26 participants in the 2008 New York Marathon were over age 80. I've also read about over-80 softball players, which is particularly inspirational to me because I play softball every Sunday in the spring and summer (and a bunch of the guys I play with are well into their sixties). People lose muscle mass, strength, flexibility, and bone density as they age, which leads to frailty, a loss of mobility, and, as a result, a loss independence. Jane Brody, in one of her *New York Times* columns, explained that this can be countered with regular participation in aerobics, strength training, and balance and flexibility exercises. The key thing, she wrote, is to start slowly and build gradually — which should sound familiar to you by now. (Brody also suggests obtaining guidance from a fitness professional, because, as my experience attests, it's important to be sure that you are doing exercises correctly, both to obtain the maximum benefit and to avoid injury.)

✳ Getting Started

Dr. Weil regularly publishes smart, simple recommendations on starting a fitness routine. He recommends starting small (there it is again!): taking the stairs at work every other day, working out with light weights, or using an exercise bike for a few minutes. He counsels that we shouldn't worry if we are going slower than others, which is a hugely important suggestion.

Other people's workouts have nothing to do with yours. Not only that, but if you're at a gym where you feel self-conscious about what you're doing, you should find another gym where the atmosphere is supportive.

You should do whatever you need to do to help you to start, and to stay with, a routine. As I've discussed, I love to read while I exercise, but of course you can also watch TV or movies to help you get through your workouts. Do whatever works best for you. Gyms almost always have TVs. These days, they often have a TV screen for each piece of exercise equipment. I read in the *Wall Street Journal* that more innovations are coming: on-demand videos, television shows, news, and e-mail access. I often use the time I spend exercising at home to catch up on all the movies and TV shows I've been wanting to watch — whether on DVD, DVR, and even VHS. I've been doing that more often over the past couple of years while I stretch or lift weights. I'll watch one episode of a show during each workout, or I'll watch a movie, section by section, over the course of a week. My friend Sharon says that she can't wait to exercise each day because she looks forward to listening to podcasts she regularly downloads to her iPod.

Once you do get into an exercise routine, keep the momentum going. And don't let the weather get in your way. My wife and I walk almost all year round. New York area winters do not regularly feature single-digit or below-zero temperatures, but they certainly meet most people's definition of cold. We dress warmly and once we start walking, we're removing layers. An article in *Best Life* magazine said that in cold weather, you can work out harder without feeling it as much as you otherwise would — likely in part because when the weather is cooler, you can stay comfortable at higher intensities (and as a result, you'll burn more calories).

✳ Exercise Even When You Have a Cold

I almost never skip a day of exercise, even if I'm not 100 percent well. I never researched whether it was good, bad, or neutral to work out when I have a cold; I did it mostly to avoid losing momentum. Then I happened upon a couple of articles on the subject. In one of her "Personal Best" columns in the *New York Times*, Gina Kolata wrote that research had led experts to recommend exercise for people with colds, although they were more cautious for conditions that produce fevers or chest congestion. She also made the point that people often fall away from their exercise programs entirely after taking time off due to a cold or some other reason — the same concern I had for many years regarding interruptions in my exercise routine.

Dr. Jordan Metzl, a sports-medicine specialist at the Hospital for Special Surgery in New York City, addressed the issue in *Best Life*'s "Ask the Fitness Coach" column, saying that exercising with a mild cold can potentially speed up your recovery, but recommending against exercise if you have a fever of more than 101 degrees. (All that said, because I'm not a doctor, I suggest consulting your physician for advice.)

On a similar note, when I'm injured I figure out how to keep exercising while avoiding the injured body part. If I hurt my foot and can't run on the treadmill, I'll ride the exercise bike every day until I can go back to alternating. I'll also avoid some weight-lifting exercises when I have certain conditions — for example, when I had tendonitis in one arm (aka tennis elbow). I play sports, so injuries will happen — though most of my aches seem to come not from sports, but from doing something dumb like reaching for something in an awkward way. I work hard to rehab, religiously following whatever routine is recommended to me by physical therapists, podiatrists, or anyone else who helps me when I'm injured. I write down exactly what the physical therapist tells me to do,

I ask for printed illustrations or I draw pictures, and I incorporate new stretches into my routine to strengthen the affected area and help to stay flexible.

Being physically fit will help you recover faster from injuries or surgery. My dad had that experience. In late 2007, he had to have his gallbladder removed. Gallbladder surgery is often performed laparoscopically, and recovery is much faster and less painful after laparoscopic surgery than after traditional open surgery, but my dad had to have the open surgery. My mom, my siblings, and I went with my dad for a presurgery meeting. The doctor told my dad that he would recover much faster because he exercised regularly. My dad asked, "Should I slow down my routine before the surgery, as the date gets closer?" The doctor said, "No, do more. Do as much as you can."

✳ A Few Final Words on Exercise

Here are a few good articles for you to read:

- On muscle-building and weight-lifting routines: http://www. intense-workout.com/muscle_building.html.

- On remembering to stick with exercise for the long term: "Fitness Isn't an Overnight Sensation," by Gina Kolata of the *New York Times.*

- On having a gym at home: "4 Ways to Start a Home Gym," by Dr. Weil, and "With the Right Motivation, That Home Gym Makes Sense," by Tara Parker-Pope of the *New York Times.*

- For a good review of the recommended amounts and types of exercise: "Fit, Not Frail: Exercise as a Tonic for Aging," by Jane Brody of the *New York Times.*

I've talked a lot about how I do it. The goal here is for *you* to do it, whichever way works best for you. Whether or not you copy what I do, whether you do it in the morning or at night, whether you do it at home or in a gym, it's all good. Be healthy. Exercise.

Be Healthy, Part 3: Beyond Eating Well and Exercising

✳ Wellness

Marianne Morano, a clinical exercise physiologist, gave an informative presentation to my company on wellness. She explained that 70 percent of medical costs are for diseases related to lifestyle choices, and that you can decrease your risk for disease and increase the quality and length of life with certain behaviors. I asked her for a short list of recommendations. In addition to exercise and eating well, here are her suggestions (not in any particular order):

- Don't smoke.

- Go for an annual physical that includes a blood pressure test and a full blood workup (checking your cholesterol, blood sugar, etc.).

- Maintain a regular sleep schedule with seven to eight hours of sleep each night.

- Always wear a seat belt, whether you are the driver or the passenger.

- Regularly practice stress-reduction techniques.

- Do not drink more than one to two alcoholic drinks per day.

Marianne doesn't suggest extreme behavior. Moderation is a tenet of her program. While she suggests avoiding fat and white flour, she will be the first to tell you that you should have a piece of cake at a party. She explains that you can't change your age, your heredity, or the fact that you were born a certain gender (I said it that way on purpose, meaning people may have procedures to change genders, but they can't change how they were born or what impact their birth gender will have on their health).

What you can change are your habits: you can assess your health, you can quit smoking, you can pay attention to what you eat, and you can exercise daily. If you don't find time for exercise and you don't eat well, you'll have to find the time for illness, instead of enjoying your wellness. Here are some additional thoughts on wellness.

✳ Please Quit Smoking

It's gotten harder to be a smoker. You can't smoke in many public places — airplanes, offices, restaurants, bars. Nonsmokers look at you in a not-so-nice way when you light up. I know that many smokers feel strongly about their rights and say that their right to smoke has been stomped on by (to them) an overzealous, health-obsessed, secondhand-smoke-fearing public, and politicians who only care about being reelected. But there's a reason for all of this. Smoking is a proven killer. It causes cancer, heart disease, and other serious health problems. I don't want to get into a fight with the smokers of the world. I just want to plead with you to quit — for your benefit and also for your family's benefit. I urge you to try any and every way to break the habit — nicotine patches, nicotine gum, hypnosis, cold turkey, whatever it takes. Maybe you need a mantra to repeat to yourself every time you're about to light up. Here's one for you: *Mind over matches.*

I feel lucky that I never had a desire to try a cigarette. I have two vivid smoking-related memories from my childhood. One incident occurred after my grandmother died of a heart attack when I was 5 years old. When I asked my mother why she died, my mom replied, "She smoked when she was younger." Whether my mom was just simplifying for me or was trying to send a message, or both, the message was received. The other memory is of an antismoking exhibit that we had at our elementary school every year. Each class had a turn to walk through it. What has always stuck with me are the cotton lungs. There was an acrylic torso filled with cotton, representing the lungs. The left lung, representing a nonsmoker, was beautiful, made up of clean, white, puffy cotton. The right lung, into which cigarette smoke was being piped, was black and gray, dirty, sooty, and shriveling. It was powerful.

I stupidly had a stint using smokeless tobacco. In high school, my friend Chris introduced me and a couple of other friends to Copenhagen and Skoal. We did as the tobacco ads instructed — "just a pinch between your cheek and gum" — and then walked around town spitting out tobacco juice and feeling like we were pretty cool. We also liked to have the round tobacco tin's circle visible in the back pocket of our jeans. No one told us chewing tobacco was bad for you — though I never considered telling my parents that I was doing it, so I knew I was doing something wrong. We got a wake-up call about smokeless tobacco before it became a tragedy. Chris shocked us all one day when he told us he was quitting. "I have to," he said. "I just came from the doctor with my mom and dad. The doctor says I have a precancerous growth in my mouth. He said it's definitely from the chaw." We all quit cold turkey.

I wish grown-ups could take the wake-up call as easily as we kids did. All of us know, or know of, people who have died of smoking-related diseases. I have often wondered whether the fact that chain-smokers can make it across the country on a six-hour flight from New York to California is a sign that anyone can stop if they do it in small steps. When a sports team is down three games to none in a seven-game series, the coach will say something like, "We just have to win tonight's game. After that, we can talk about the next step." They know they have to win four games, but the only one they can do anything about is the game they're about to play. It's not about winning four games. It's about winning one game, then winning one game, then winning one game, then winning one game. In the same way, how about stopping smoking for an hour? Then another hour. Then another. When you've made it for one day, keep at it for a second day. Keep adding days until you get to a week. Keep adding weeks until you get to a month. Keep adding months until you get to a year. We all know people who have quit. I have many friends who quit. Try it. *Mind over matches.*

✳ Please Get a Checkup

In addition to laws that limit where you can smoke, New York City has legislated against restaurants serving trans fats. Talking on a cell phone while driving, unless it's hands-free, has become illegal in many places. So why not pass laws mandating checkups? (Or exercise, for that matter?) One reason is that those ideas are tougher to police. They are "start" behaviors, as opposed to "stops." Even the law requiring you to wear a seat belt is really a law saying, "No driving without a seat belt."

In addition to a comprehensive annual physical, with screenings for diseases that run in your family, you should keep a journal of your medical history, including family history, and adopt appropriate preventive lifestyle behaviors.

At the start of this chapter, I talked about the wonderful medical advances that have allowed people, including relatives and friends of mine, to survive diseases that used to be death sentences. Sadly, other friends of mine have died way too young from cancer. One was my friend Ellen, who was diagnosed with stage IV colon cancer at the age of 40. Ellen passed away in 2010, after a brave and grueling three-year battle with the disease. Ellen kept a journal on CaringBridge.org, where family and friends were able to keep up with her fight and post messages of encouragement to Ellen and her family. Each March, Ellen posted a note to promote Colorectal Cancer Awareness Month and made this plea: "PLEASE be screened if you are 50 or older OR are younger but have any unexplained gastrointestinal symptoms OR have a family history of colorectal cancer. Also, please use this month to remind friends and family to do the same. Colonoscopies — the gold standard in screening — are not painful or difficult. Best of all, even if there is a problem, if it's found early, it can often be remedied right then at the colonoscopy. Please do not wait." In another post, Ellen, who was thin her whole life, wrote: "As you all now know, it is NOT just a disease of overweight older men. Colorectal cancer is the second-leading cause of death from cancer in the US (after lung cancer). But if caught EARLY it is almost always curable, and the screening test itself can often PREVENT cancer by removing polyps that could become cancerous. If you are over 50 or if you have any history at all of colorectal cancer in your family, please get a colonoscopy. SOON. It really is not so bad. But discovering colon cancer at a late stage is."

The earlier you find out that something is wrong, the better chance you have to deal with it before it becomes a major problem. It's like your car. There's a reason why the manufacturer's warranty can be voided if you don't follow the maintenance schedule outlined in the owner's manual. The company is willing to guarantee the car's performance *if* you do your part. They know that if you don't take care of your car, if you don't get it routinely checked, it will break down prematurely. It's the same with our bodies. Keep getting those 3,000-mile checkups on your car and keep getting that annual physical on your most important machine — your body.

✳ Get Enough Sleep

I know that different people seem to need different amounts of sleep, but you should try to average at least seven hours. This is sometimes a struggle for me. I never have trouble falling asleep; my problem is that I rarely can sleep late. I'm used to rising early, so on work days my body clock often wakes me up just before my alarm goes off, and on weekends I usually wake up at that same hour.

But I *like* being an early riser. I get a ton done, including exercise, early in the morning while everyone else is asleep.

I also feel that waking up early can be a good sign about one's frame of mind. It's something I first realized with my son when he was in elementary school. Jeremy was staying up late on weeknights and needed to be up early for school the next day. He also got up early on weekends — even as he got older and would stay out late the night before. Marcie would worry that he wasn't getting enough sleep. I was concerned too, but he seemed fine. His health was good, and his disposition wasn't sour. One day, as Marcie and I were talking about his sleeping habits, it hit me: The kid stays up late and wakes up early for one reason — he likes to be awake. That's a good thing. He enjoys life. He likes extending each day as long as he can by staying up late, and he likes resuming his enjoyment by getting up early the next morning. And it hit me that I'm the same way.

Because I always wake up early, the only way I can be sure to get a lot of sleep is to go to sleep early. Of course, I find it hard to get to bed early, because there's so much I want to do each night. But getting those extra hours of rest is important for my mind and body.

One more thing about sleep: While there's no cure for the common cold, I've found that two things will shorten the duration of my colds — sleep and drinking plenty of fluids. When I have a cold, I make an extra effort to go to bed early. I also drink tons of water, enough so that my urine is totally clear (but I have to be careful to stop early enough in the evening so that I don't wake up during the night to go to the bathroom). Also, I've read that running short on sleep can substantially increase the risk of catching a cold because your body and your immune system are weakened.

✳ Always Wear Your Seat Belt

I'm old enough to remember when we didn't wear seat belts. Not only did I not wear a seat belt when I was a kid, but my favorite seat in the back of the car was the middle seat (despite the hump that cut into my leg room). I loved leaning forward to talk with my parents. The front passenger seat is sometimes called the "death seat" because it's considered to be the most dangerous place to be sitting in the event of an accident. I was definitely in a "death seat" as well, and I'm fortunate that I wasn't hurt or killed in a car accident.

Why didn't we wear seat belts? We just didn't. The ironic thing is that seat belts were much less annoying back then. We didn't have shoulder belts (an important safety improvement that came later and that was first introduced only in the front seats). All we had were lap belts, and in the backseat, where we usually sat as kids, those were left buried in the crack behind the seat cushion.

By the time I was driving, my parents were regularly wearing seat belts in the front of the car. They taught me that the first thing you do when you get into the car is buckle your seat belt. It quickly became automatic for me.

When states started passing laws requiring the use of seat belts, many people objected. My enterprising and sometimes authority-defying younger brother looked to cash in on the unhappiness by creating seat belt T-shirts — they had a shoulder seat belt printed on them to make it look like you were wearing a seat belt when you were driving. He didn't sell too many from the stand that he set up in front of his college dorm at

New York University in Manhattan, and we had quite a supply of those shirts for years after.

Meanwhile, the facts are indisputable: Wearing a seat belt reduces your chance of serious injury and death. It's simply a terrible decision to not wear a seat belt *every* time you're in a car, whether you're the driver or a passenger.

Still, many people choose not to wear a seat belt. A 2009 U.S. Department of Transportation study estimated that 1,652 lives could be saved and 22,372 serious injuries avoided each year if seat-belt use rates rose to 90 percent in every state. Seat-belt use is particularly low among teenagers. Federal statistics show that more teens are killed by traffic accidents than by any other cause, including any disease, and more than half of the 4,540 teens killed in car accidents in 2007 were not wearing seat belts.

✳ Drinking and Driving

I'm going to spend just a brief moment on DUI (driving under the influence) or DWI (driving while intoxicated). It's even more stupid than driving without a seat belt, and it's totally unacceptable. Even though this book is focused on how you can help yourself, I'm going to say this about the difference between seat-belt use and DUI: If you want to risk killing yourself by driving without a seat belt, that's up to you. But if you want to risk killing yourself by driving under the influence, that's not your choice, because you can kill others at the same time — your passengers, passengers in other cars, pedestrians, runners or cyclists, people eating in sidewalk cafés, etc. It's incredible to me that anyone drives drunk. Okay, I'm done.

✳ Driving While Drowsy

DWD (driving while drowsy) gets far less publicity than DWI, but it, too, is a killer. Experts strongly urge you to stop driving if you experience extremely tired eyes (you have difficulty keeping your eyes open or focusing); if you're weaving (straying outside of your lane or onto the rumble strips); or if you lose track of time or can't remember the last stretch of road. The experts warn that cool air, loud music, and caffeine won't keep you awake; instead, find a safe place to pull over, and take a short nap. A great article by Bengt Halverson covers the important issue of DWD (you can find the article on the Car Connection Web site). To minimize the chances of becoming drowsy behind the wheel, Halverson recommends getting a full night of sleep before traveling, moderating your sugar intake, stopping every two hours for a break, and bringing a companion. The article also lists signals of excessive fatigue to look for in the driver when you're a passenger.

✳ Driving While Texting

DWT (driving while texting) is now illegal in most places — thank goodness. You can't be looking at the road and at the phone at the same time. As I wrote in Chapter 2, you can't do *any* two things at the same time and give full attention to both. People think they can. But we can't. There are some activities that we routinely do together, but it's usually a bad idea. We eat and talk at the same time, which can cause you to choke. We eat while watching TV, which causes weight gain because we don't pay attention to how much we're eating.

If someone walks into your office and you type on your computer while talking to them, you're being rude and breaking the "Be Nice" rule. If you drive while texting, you're breaking the "Be Healthy" rule. So many accidents have happened because of DWT. In 2009, a Boston trolley operator ran a red light while text-messaging his girlfriend. Forty-nine people were injured when he crashed into another trolley. Before that incident, Boston transit employees were prohibited from using cell phones while working. Subsequently, trolley operators were barred from even carrying a cell phone while on duty. The myth of multitasking once again comes into play here. When you are texting, you are giving all of your attention to texting. Yes, you might be doing something else "at the same time," but actually you are bouncing back and forth between the two activities. And with driving, even one second doing something else can have deadly consequences. Do not text while you drive. Do not read texts you receive. Do not reply to ones you receive. Do not initiate text conversations.

✳ More Driving Tips

I read an excellent summary of safe driving tips in my kids' high school newspaper, *The Northern Star*. Reporter Kyla Cheung provided the following safe driving suggestions, which she collected from the school' students and staff: don't drive tired (sleeping six to seven hours makes drivers twice as likely to be involved in a crash as sleeping eight hours); don't use your phone when you drive; don't drive too fast (don't be afraid to go the speed limit, even if somebody is close behind you); clean the snow off your car, remembering the top of your car (flying sheets of ice pose a hazard to drivers behind you); don't rush (allow yourself double the time you need); stop at stop signs (as opposed to rolling through them); pay attention to the road; be careful when roads are wet or icy; don't drive with boots, heels, or sandals; and practice defensive driving.

✳ Wear a Bike Helmet

Please wear a helmet when you ride a bike. You're sharing the road with large, heavy vehicles. And any bicycle accident, whether or not it involves a vehicle, can cause life-threatening head injuries. I see many people riding without a helmet. I grew up never wearing a helmet. I'm not even sure they existed in the 1960 and '70s. But I always wear one now. And please make sure to strap it on. Wearing a helmet with the chin strap not buckled is practically useless because the helmet will almost surely go flying off your head if you go flying off the bike.

✳ Cell Phones and Cancer?

I don't know whether cell phone use causes cancer, but I've been using earbuds (like the ones you use with an iPod, but with a small microphone attached to the wire) for most of the time that I've had a cell phone. While I do it mainly for the convenience of being able to talk on the phone without holding it up to my ear, a part of me does it just in case cell phones can cause cancer. With the earbuds, at least the phone is not right next to my head. There is no proven connection between cell phone use and cancer (though more and more studies point to a possible link), but I figure, why take the chance? *Best Life* quoted neurosurgeon and scientist Keith L. Black, MD, as saying that he always uses an earpiece with his cell phone to lower his risk of developing brain cancer.

My kids quickly became heavy cell phone users, and I used to urge them to use the speakerphone feature — though that wasn't always practical — and to save their longer conversations for our home phone. Before too long, however, they made the switch from calling to primarily texting — a change I welcomed. I may have to worry about them injuring their thumbs from the extreme amount of texting they do (seriously), but I'll take that over concerns about cancer.

✳ Stress

Plenty has been written about the effect stress has on our health. Numerous studies indicate that psychological stress can take a physical toll on our bodies' systems, and experts suggest exercise, regular and balanced meals, adequate sleep, social connections, and therapy as some of the ways to keep stress under control. Exercise causes our bodies to release endorphins, natural feel-good chemicals, and the effects can last for hours. It's amazing how it all comes together. The things we've been talking about — exercise, eating well, sleep — that are so important for your physical health are also extremely important for your mental well-being.

Therapy is an important way to deal with stress. So many of us grew up in a culture that stigmatized taking care of your mental well-being. "Mental illness" has the word "illness" in it is because it's just as much an illness as any other and deserves to be treated with the same consideration, care, and seriousness. Mental illnesses or any other kinds of psychological concerns are not flaws or faults. They are conditions, and we all need to be comfortable getting professional help for them. If for some reason you don't want to go to someone you think of as a psychologist, psychiatrist, therapist, or the like, don't think of them by those names. Instead, think of them as life coaches — after all, that's what they are, someone coaching you on living your life.

Also, talk with family and friends and maintain social connections. Dr. Weil and many other health experts regularly tout the important benefits of human interaction. In *The Happiness Hypothesis*, Jonathan Haidt cites studies showing that when people have strong social relationships, the immune system is strengthened, life is extended, and recovery from surgery is accelerated. There is also evidence that having social connections reduces the risks of depression and anxiety disorders. And when we help one another, the benefits go both ways. Haidt writes that there is research showing that it's even more beneficial to care for others than to receive help.

I've made maintaining social connections a priority. Like everything else, if you don't put it on your schedule, you won't do it, because you inevitably get caught up in all your other activities. After Marcie and

I had children and "settled down" in the suburbs, I became frustrated that we rarely saw our best friends — after I had spent so much time with friends during my childhood, my college years, and my early adult years. In a deliberate attempt to fix that, we created a dinner club among five couples. Each couple hosts the other four couples twice a year for a Saturday night dinner. Suddenly we had plans for 10 nights a year with our best friends — whom we had been seeing only a couple of times a year. I have other friends I would like to do that with as well — I would love to have two dinner clubs going, and maybe someday I will.

An article in *Prevention* listed these additional ways to cut your level of stress: meditation; listening to music; sipping black tea; hanging out with a funny friend or watching a funny TV show or movie; getting a massage; doing something spiritual; and chewing gum. Regarding the spiritual part, the article suggests that people who are not interested in organized religion can try walking in nature or volunteering for a charity.

Haidt says meditation is like a free, all-natural pill that, if taken once a day, reduces anxiety and increases contentment, self-esteem, empathy and trust, with no negative side effects. In Chapter 1, I talked about the breathing exercise I learned in yoga classes, which I've used to help myself fall back asleep in the middle of the night. I slowly, completely exhale through my mouth, counting to at least eight, then I slowly breathe in through my nose, counting to four. (There's a bit more to the "official" version of yogic breathing, and if you want to learn it, take up yoga — which I definitely recommend. In the meantime, doing it this way is perfectly fine.) I taught my children yogic breathing to help them fall asleep when they were sick or for whatever reason were up in the middle of the night and came to me crying, "I've been up for two hours; I'll never fall back asleep." The breathing exercise works because you can't think of more than one thing at a time, and if you're focusing on your monotonous breathing then it pushes other distractions out of your mind. And taking long, deep breaths is an oft-recommended stress-reduction and relaxation technique.

Best Life had an article that provided "10 quick ways to stress less." The article saved the best for last, revealing that Scottish researchers found that having sex regularly lowers anxiety, stress, and blood pressure.

❋ Completely Disconnected Time Off From Work

Another important stress-reduction technique is taking time off from work. A lot of people go on vacation but bring work with them. That's more prevalent than ever these days with all our electronic devices. People will tell me, "I'm going away next week and I'm not checking my e-mails…except early in the morning when my family is sleeping, then again at 4 pm." While that's a thousand times better than not taking a vacation, I recommend completely disconnecting on your days off, as I discussed in the introduction. That's what I do. On workdays, I work. On other days, I don't.

You can't totally control which thoughts come to your mind, so sometimes I can't avoid thinking about work. If it's something I want to follow up on, I write it down or leave myself a voice mail at work, and forget about it until the next workday. Otherwise, I'm 100 percent off. When I read on days off, I read for pleasure. When I talk with friends, it's not about work. It's rejuvenating, which is incredibly important.

Days off are important, and just like all the other important activities we talked about in Chapter 4, if you don't schedule them, they won't happen. In one of Sue Shellenbarger's excellent *Work & Family* columns in the *Wall Street Journal*, she reported on her own successful personal experiment, completely disconnecting from work for at least one weekend day. She explained that the better days off helped her to have better results at work. I've had the same experience.

✳ Vitamins

The best way to get the nutrients we all need is through food. Because it's nearly impossible to make sure we are eating everything we need to, supplementing the food is sometimes necessary, and a trip to a nutritionist and your physician for recommendations is important.

I take a multivitamin and vitamin D. Vitamin D is being touted as a super-vitamin that can help prevent all types of ailments, including some cancers. The most common way to get vitamin D is to spend time in the sun, without the protection of sunscreen. Because we're so careful these days about how much time we spend in the sun, due to the dangers of skin cancer, and because many of us live in climates where there is not enough sunshine during the year to give us the amount of vitamin D we need, vitamin D deficiency is common. Again, I'm not a doctor. Please consult your physician before taking any vitamins or supplements.

✳ Sun Protection

Remember when sunscreen was called suntan lotion? Those days are long gone. My father and my brother have both had skin cancer removed, so I am acutely aware of the need to be protected from the sun. Jane Brody has frequently written in her column about the sun protection essentials: wear clothes that block much of the sun's radiation; apply a complete sunscreen throughout the day every day; and stay out of the midday sun as much as possible. I try to do all these things. Plus I go for annual screenings at a dermatologist. Others go more frequently.

The article by Camille Noe Pagan that I mentioned earlier ("You Don't Need to Be a Health Perfectionist") says that the gold standard of sun protection is to apply SPF 30 or higher several times a day, and that SPF 15 is "good enough." I almost always use 30 or higher. I also make sure the label says "Broad Spectrum UVA/UVB," indicating that it protects against both types of harmful rays. Ask a dermatologist for a recommendation when you get that checkup I talked about.

I've read that melanoma skin cancers can be caused by a single sunburn. I wear a hat almost all the time when I'm in the sun, though I don't necessarily wear a broad-brimmed hat as is recommended, and I make sure to apply sunscreen to my face, neck, and ears. I don't wear a hat when I'm swimming (wearing a bathing cap is recommended), but I try not to swim during the hottest parts of the day. (Note: I am bald, so sunscreen on my head is essential. Even if you're not bald, parts of your scalp can get burned if you're not careful. When I spend time in the sun for my vitamin D, I wear a hat and keep my head in the shade — sitting at the edge of the shade of an umbrella.) Sunglasses with UV protection are also frequently recommended.

As mentioned, it *is* important to spend some time in the sun, unprotected by sunscreen, in order to get vitamin D. I read a great article on the subject by Martin Mittelstaedt in Toronto's *Globe and Mail* newspaper. In it, John Cannell, head of the Vitamin D Council, a nonprofit, California-based organization, recommends taking a bit of a chance by spending some time unprotected in the sun. He presents the excellent logic that 1,500 Americans die every year from skin cancers, while 1,500 Americans die every *day* from other major cancers.

I have read a variety of recommendations on this issue, many of which say we need as little as a few minutes of sun exposure two or three times a week during the summer months. Again, ask your dermatologist.

✳ Brain Exercise

In Chapter 5 I focused on the importance of being a lifelong learner. I will add here that lifelong learning is not just for personal development

— it's also vital for your health. You must keep your brain active, whether it's through reading, doing crossword or Sudoku puzzles, or performing other mental exercises. Keep learning, and keep exercising your brain.

✳ Stay Alive!

We periodically see articles about people who have lived past the age of 100. I'm privileged to know the family of one of those people. In early 2009, I went to the funeral of Berta Rosenberg, who was 112 when she passed away. Berta, known as Omi to her family, was the great-grandmother of a friend of my kids. Omi was very "with it" until about age 104. People are staying alive!

An article in *Esquire* titled "The World's Healthiest 75-Year-Old Man" told of Don Wildman, who runs, snowboards, and bikes. Wildman says, "When you stop moving, it's all over." He retired at 61 because working made it hard for him to reach his goal of snowboarding 100 days a year. He likes hanging out with people much younger than he is because they think they're going to live forever and he finds that thinking contagious. If you're going to live a long time, there's another reason to hang out with young people: You'll need people who will be around in your later years. Yogi Berra's granddaughter, Lindsay, told the *New York Times* that Yogi sometimes says that he threw away his address book because "everyone in it is dead."

Whenever I think about living long enough to live forever, I hear Daniel Day-Lewis as Hawkeye in *The Last of the Mohicans* telling the beautiful Cora Munro (played by Madeleine Stowe) to go with her captors rather than fight and risk death, and imploring her to "stay alive!" No matter what happens, he says, he will find her. I keep hearing him yelling at her, "Stay alive!" and I like that mantra for wellness.

My brother wrote in *The Special Needs Parent Handbook*: "I once read something that really stuck with me — those who don't make time for health will have to make time for illness. While we can all come up with excuses not to exercise and take care of ourselves, the day you get really sick and you are laid up in a hospital bed, all of a sudden you have all of the time in the world to lie around. Wouldn't it be better to spend that time now making yourself healthier and having fun with your friends and family?" Because of what we know about how to take care of ourselves and because of medical advances, we can stay alive much longer — as long as we choose to make that a priority now.

Marianne Morano told me about the "Wellness Continuum," which runs from premature death to optimal health. While no one would choose premature death, we do make choices all the time that determine where we end up on the spectrum, and some of those choices lead to premature death. When Morano told me this, it reminded me of the way parents-to-be sometimes express a desire for a boy or a girl, and then add, "But I don't really care, as long as it's healthy." Being healthy is the *most important thing* when we're born. It should be the most important thing every day of our lives. Let's make being healthy a lifelong priority. Please keep reminding yourself: Be healthy. Stay alive.

✳ New Habits and Progress

Remember: *Life is long*, meaning we have time. If we try to make a million changes all at once, we often end up so overwhelmed that we make none. Instead, if we *slow down to make the changes*, and then *stop to celebrate the progress*, we'll accomplish much more.

Slow Down to Make the Changes — It takes 21 days to form a new habit. What are some ideas you have for new habits you would like to adopt following your reading of Chapter 6?

Stop to Celebrate the Progress — Remember to look back on all that you've accomplished. What are some areas of progress you've made?

Conclusion

"The Self-Improvement of Salvadore Ross" is one of my favorite episodes from *The Twilight Zone* TV series. In that episode, Ross discovers that he has a magical ability to improve his life by making unusual trades with others — trading a frustrating broken hand for a minor respiratory infection, for example, and trading his youth for wealth. This power enables him to achieve the self-improvement required to successfully woo the woman he desires. I won't play spoiler, other than to say that because he's in the Twilight Zone, where surprise endings and unintended consequences are the rule, Ross experiences complications en route to his ultimate goal.

While we don't have the ability to make magical trades for self-improvement, we do have the ability to change — to become happier, healthier, and more fulfilled. And unlike with *The Twilight Zone* bargains, the only price we have to pay is putting in the reasonable effort that it takes to create new habits. In most cases, the changes don't even require extra time. We just have to make a decision that we want to change, followed by a 21-day commitment to implementing that change.

Every business guru advises us to break down work goals into smaller pieces, and yet for some reason (probably related to our culture of instant gratification), we aren't taught to apply that advice to our personal lives. We won't see a TV commercial that goes like this: "Hi, I'm Jim and I made 52 positive changes to my life. Can you believe that? You can, too, in just *three short years!*"

Instead, we try and fail to achieve oversize goals or we don't try at all because these giant goals are too intimidating — which is precisely why breaking down our goals into smaller pieces is the key.

While the six rules are simple, they're not easy if you try to tackle them all at once like a set of New Year's resolutions. Slowing down — breaking up your desired life improvements into specific habits that you can adopt one 21-day period at a time — is what makes change achievable.

And because we won't be seeing TV commercials advertising "slow fixes," we have to remind ourselves that we have the great gift of time. That we can break down our goals into smaller pieces because *life is long*. That we need to *slow down to make the changes*, and then *stop to celebrate the progress*, in order to accomplish much more. And that the time's going to go by anyway, so why not make our lives better along the way?

We can do this!

✳ Keep in Touch

In my blog posts I'm going to share my own ongoing changes as well as other resources, stories, and suggestions — including ones from people like you who join the "Six Simple Rules" community, where life is long and continuous improvement is celebrated and encouraged.

I can't wait to hear about your progress and your great ideas for a better life and a better world for us all.

Acknowledgements

One secret to a better life is having wonderful family members and friends, and I've been blessed with many, including quite a few whom I would call BFFs (borrowing a term from my daughters). Encouragement (a word I'm going to use many times in these acknowledgments) is one of the many priceless gifts that I am incredibly fortunate to receive from them.

Thank you to Josh Tycko, Claudia Zurlini, Farah Shanock, Tracie Rosenbaum, and Jeff Wilson for early, positive feedback and encouragement, which are great confidence boosters.

Thank you to Michael Friedman, Alan Siegel, Ross Slater, and Jane Rubin for advice.

Thank you to Adam Savetsky for your excellent input and encouragement.

I've paid tribute to my parents by writing about them and I'd also like to thank them here, along with all the other people I wrote about who have inspired and influenced me.

Thank you to Dan Sullivan, whose influence I have documented, as well as Babs Smith, Shannon Waller, Catherine Nomura, Susan Aldridge, Ken Arlen, Colleen O'Donnell, our discussion group, my fellow workshop participants, and everyone else associated with the Strategic Coach®, past and present.

Thank you to everyone I work with at Singer Nelson Charlmers. A special shout-out to Evelyn, who has helped me keep my notes organized.

Ron Drenger is a wonderful editor. He provided all that I expected in the way of grammar corrections and similar tweaks, as well as so much that I hadn't expected by challenging me to make the book better with his insightful suggestions. I was lucky to find him. (Thanks, Sharon.)

Joseph Manghise is a fantastic copy editor and proofreader. I was lucky to find him. (Thanks, Rob.)

Sharon Schanzer, who is a great friend and seems able to do almost anything, offered all kinds of help and advice when I first told her about the book, because that's just how she is. Much later, I hired her to create my beautiful Web site, manage this book project, and design the book, and she taught me quite a bit along the way.

My best friends, business partners, and blood and non-blood brothers, Jonathan Singer and Mark Shanock, provided terrific suggestions and encouragement from the first draft to the galleys. And I must include a shameless plug for the amazing and inspiring work Jon has done to make the world a better place for individuals with autism (and their families) through charitable endeavors to support research, education, and advocacy. Learn more at drive4rebecca.org.

I'm eternally grateful for the encouragement and mentoring of my fantastic friend Robert Edelstein. In 1987, Rob sat with me at his kitchen table in Queens, New York, helping with the manuscript of my (unpublished) first book. Twenty-two years later, we were back at his kitchen table, this time in New Jersey, as he provided priceless guidance for this book. And he gave me plenty of encouragement and positive feedback in between. (Shameless plug No. 2: Read Rob's books. My favorite is *Full Throttle*, Rob's biography of legendary NASCAR driver Curtis Turner, which was favorably reviewed in the *New York Times*.)

It was a special moment for me when my son, Jeremy, read a late draft of the introduction, made a few notes on it, and wrote on the bottom, "Very Good," like a teacher grading a student. Jeremy has encouraged me and provided me with great editorial commentary — and he has taught me so much starting on the day he was born.

My daughters, Julie and Cara, have enabled me to see a bit through female eyes by trusting me when I told them they could tell me anything. Helping others is a key to happiness, and it comes naturally to Julie and Cara. They are lucky to have that gift, and the world is fortunate to benefit from it.

To my wife, Marcie, thank you for allowing me to (continue to) learn on the job (and to write about some of it). As I've said before, in public, thanks to you I've been able to live the life of my dreams.

About the Author

David J. Singer is the co-founder and CEO of Singer Nelson Charlmers, an insurance firm in the New York City area. For many years, David served as a role-model speaker for Directions for Our Youth, a program for inner-city high school students. Each semester, David conducted workshops for 150 or so ninth- and 10th-graders to help them learn secrets to success, sharing some of the advice that turned into *Six Simple Rules for a Better Life*. David was also involved with a New York City high school as part of PENCIL'S "Principal for a Day" program.

David's drive to make the world a better place is the reason he wrote *Six Simple Rules for a Better Life*. He has coached his kids' sports teams, chaperoned their school trips, written reviews on parenting books, served on committees for the board of education, and served as a board member for a local community institution. David lectures for companies on *Six Simple Rules for a Better Life* and writes the *Six Simple Rules for a Better Life* blog.

David was mentored in his writing by Robert Edelstein, author of several books, including *Full Throttle*, which was reviewed on the cover of the *New York Times Book Review*. *Six Simple Rules for a Better Life* is David's first book.

SixSimpleRules.com
david@SixSimpleRules.com
Twitter: @sixsimplerules
Facebook: http://www.facebook.com/SixSimpleRules

Made in the USA
Charleston, SC
12 November 2011